Ars Aurora

The Beatitudes of Christ

A sacred guide to inner healing in the
words of the beloved Lord Jesus

Copyright © 2024 Ars Aurora

N.: 312251344

WWW.WORKSCOPYRIGHT.COM

I thank my beloved Lord Jesus Christ. For granting me this opportunity to evolve and spread his kind light on this Earth.

I thank all my guides, mentors, holy Angels and Archangels and all the blessed souls who sustain my life on this plane, without you, none of this would be possible.

Summary

Foreword

Welcome, dear souls! I bring you something different from previous works. We are beginning to understand that everything around us is made up of vibration. We can tune in to frequencies that lift us up or that depress our souls. A new light will hover over the world, and in that light, we can find and tune in to situations from the past, in words shrouded in great love and wisdom. And bring those words to us here and now. And connecting with the essence of what was said. By recovering the past, we access the frequencies of those words and once again bring the divine reward from heaven in the words of the Beloved Christ to the present day.

We leave our current vibrational state and enter higher frequencies in the sacred words of Jesus. When we tune in to the Beatitudes, we enter a frequency that has been spoken for a long time and is still manifest today in the lives of many people around the

Earth. In this attunement, the universe manifests in us what we have uttered; and what we seek begins to become part of our life. When we manifest the Beatitudes internally, our world begins to transform; a new reality seems to emerge when we heal ourselves from within. The outer world is a reflection of our inner world; our vibratory pattern will shape the life we live, whether it's filled with happiness or endless problems to be faced. A soul healed of its pain, regrets, and patterns that are not connected to the Creator Source is a soul that lives fully, happily, prosperously, and abundantly in all areas of its life, be it professional, loving, family, personal, spiritual, mental, etc.

When a soul seeks healing from its pain, healing comes in many forms. These paths can manifest in a variety of ways such as: medical treatments, healing words from other people, spiritual healing, an acquaintance may invite you to a healing session, or you may simply find *"something"* that leads you to a process of deep healing.

Prayers seem to manifest very easily; you discover the power of psalms and Bible verses in your life; people and events seem to be synchronized, and everything leads you down a path to find the solution to your problem. The light manifests itself in this way, subtly through the equal hours, coincidences, words, prayers, visions, dreams, and such repetitive patterns of love, as if the universe were telling you, *"Look, here's the way! Follow this road, and you'll find what you're looking for."* We've all experienced these synchronicities, and this book will be no different. Everyone who comes to these pages has been led by spirituality to enter this work and learn about the beatitudes that reside here. In this work, we will go on a short journey back to the day when the Beloved Christ spoke the Beatitudes to afflicted souls in need of wisdom. Yes, we will be working with the wise words of the Beloved Christ. For he brought words not understood at the time, which even today, we can feel in our hearts the purity of his love.

"The Jesus I bring to you in these pages is a Jesus who predates all religions and above all human thoughts about his origin."

The Beatitudes of Christ

"Blessed are the poor in spirit, for theirs is the kingdom of heaven."

Matthew 5:3

At this time, when many see no way out, we feel as if we could touch a door that, when opened, leads us to the perfect world. To green fields, to the summer breeze, to the feeling of love and perpetual peace between nations, which are united as one. For in a world after its complete healing, there can be no separation between one brother and another. When humanity as a collective evolves, it ascends to its heavenly monads to complete its life. Monads are spiritual forms also known as our Divine Self, forms that are more evolved and closer to the creator. This is both a personal path of the soul itself in search of eternal perfection and the bond of all other souls in search of the same goal.

The path of individualism brings separation from the whole, and you can't ascend without first being connected to love. Love embraces and welcomes everyone. It is a collective and non-individualistic force that promotes the purest and most tenuous ecstasy that a human being can feel. We feel love at every point in our lives. Even those who haven't been able to feel it on their journeys know that everyone is very well loved, supported, and that all you have to do is ask—for love to fill you, for the light to be present in your lives, for your souls to be covered by the light of life and the love of Christ, the Ruby ray, the flame of purity, and all the rays of the divine Creator.

"I am the Light of the world; whoever follows me shall not walk in darkness, but shall have the light of life." - John 8:12

In this life, we can only think about how it used to be. However, our soul remembers all our life experiences, lived while we are incarnated on a physical plane, and also when we are alive in the spiritual realms of existence. When we talk about the deities we hold dear, I believe that many wish to come face to face with those who devote themselves to or have a deep appreciation for those who bring comfort to their souls. Be it Buddha, Christ, Krishna, Ganesha, Archangel Michael, Mary, Oxalá, and so on. What many people don't know is that at some point in their lives, your paths have been intertwined. Admiration and true love are built up over countless lifetimes, it's a reciprocal love and affection. For he who enlightens, also enlightens. Sincere love is present between the two of you at times when you needed some physical or spiritual support from these beloved spirits who come to you today.

And in these words, I attune you to the golden frequency of Beloved Christ and Beloved Master Nada, in a bath of ruby-golden energy that covers everyone at this moment. So that we can continue this little journey. Where each of you can tune in to the Christic energies of the Beatitudes. Where every soul that walks the path is covered by sacred energies that raise your lives, your vibrations and your souls for a great journey back home. As I write, I feel a tenuous love covering me, a sense of comfort, the energy of a warm, loving embrace.

"This is the feeling I want you all to feel in your hearts as you read this text. Choose to evolve through love, through divine grace, choose to be lights, choose to be better, choose to bathe your hearts in the golden ruby flame, choose to be filled with the holy spirit, choose to be happy, free and well-loved. Choose to be filled with divine love, choose to walk in the beatitudes, choose to be better every day, to learn from your mistakes, to make reparation from past mistakes and to be better in your essence. Between being perfect or flawed, choose to constantly improve within your evolutions, because it is the journey that brings the fruits of eternal grace and the Creator's unconditional love."

"In a ruby flame, I am the one who fills the emptiness of existences shrouded in the pain of regret, the failures of unthinking actions, and of what once caused harm to others. In unconditional love, the ruby ray vibrates, and I know that everyone wishes to be enveloped by this welcoming flame, because everyone who reads these pages wishes in your soul for the storms of flawed love to cease. Which is nothing more than that which is separated from your higher self. Everything that separates you is always harmful to your beings; nothing that separates you from love will do you any good. Nothing that separates you from respect, empathy, true love, the flames of the

creator, the brilliance of the sun, and the calm of the moon, will not raise you to any divine throne. Have balance in all your actions, the ruby flame will always be with you, from now on and forever."

Master Nada.

And in these wonderful words of the beloved divine Masters, I introduce you to the Nine Beatitudes of Christ. Accessed through the magick of their powerful sacred mantras, their divine seals and all the angelic keys that will be given to you here. Without further ado, let's get on with our reading.

Introduction

More and more, the Christic energy of perfect love is manifesting in this world. I see more and more mediums using the golden energy, intertwined with Yeshua's energy on Earth. This golden energy increasingly touches the hearts of the multitudes, awakens souls to their life missions, and increasingly liberates them from the prisons of this Earth. Prisons that are finally falling more and more.

I know that you may be feeling this, while others may not see these changes that spirituality has been talking about so much recently. I understand this, because I've been in this place of speech and vibration. It's difficult to see the change of light when our reality is so troubled that we can't see a way out of our apparent situations. However, one thing is always certain: spirituality and the forces of light do not abandon anyone who turns to them. But for that to happen, you need to take the first step of contact, whether it's to a greater or lesser degree. We need to take this step so that you can receive the light in our dense bodies, in order to change your reality with the more luminous and perfect vibrations of creation.

While I was writing this book, a lot happened in my life. And every day I realized that, as I delved into the mysteries of Christ's beatitudes, I saw that in their essence they are tools designed for the awakening and spiritual ascension of the being. Ascension is a topic that has been much discussed in recent times, and I would like to set aside a small part of this book to deal with it and clarify any doubts we may have about it.

Jesus Christ, what can we say about a man so well spoken of in this world? I can't really find words to describe Jesus; I just feel his brotherhood and deep love for me in my life. This I can testify to with an open heart and with a clear and truthful voice. For in times of great darkness, he was there to support me and to send his blessed angels to my rescue. That's why, when I saw in my life that there was no way out, I met the Christ energy, and that energy changed me completely, and for ever and ever. If we stop to feel the truth, if we stop to feel the heart of Christ, we will feel in our being the love and light that shines on him. And, by the way, it's a tremendously great light. Something you don't witness every day, and we can even spend our lives without knowing this greatness. I don't just want to magnify it, because words can't describe the experience of reality, whether it's much or little, if the essence vibrates in love, it becomes great in the face of all things.

I think of Christ as a dear brother, a kind, humble and pure soul. When we meet luminous spirits, we know the purity of their hearts. There, in this knowledge and in this coexistence, we really know what light is. Sometimes we need a turning point in our lives to understand and value things, and above all, to be able to appreciate the good times spent with the light. Since Christ is our guide, we are supported by the mentors of light, and we will always be on the right path for the evolution of our being.

When we know love, we no longer want to be separated from it. I felt love in my life when Christ touched me. This led me to write this book and to completely change the way I see this world. I dedicated myself to bringing his golden energy to this Earth, an energy so beautiful and serene to see. Infused into my being with Archangel Michael's 21-day prayer, which was the necessary change and the most powerful spiritual experience I've had in this incarnation. From it, everything was created and everything began, and for it, I am eternally grateful to Michael, and to the divine Christ and his assistants who supported me in moments of great suffering.

Christ being the great sun, even associated with our divine sun that warms and illuminates this world. His color in the radiant yellow vibration to the Gnostics. For some people, including myself, prince and planetary ruler and spirit of great wisdom. And for all who know him, a humble and dear brother of light.

In order to judge, we need to know, and in particular, this is an absolute truth that I have never seen contradicted by all those who have seen and worked together with Jesus for the good of this world. A true brother of light, perhaps, if everyone knew Jesus, they would have a different view of him, a view without the pain of his time on this earth, or the conceptions created over the ages about him. Not just about him, but in fact about all the luminous spirits, because those who know the light never forget it. Regardless of the paths they walk, the lives they live, the countless incarnations on different planets and experiences they have had. The memory of the light and of what they have lived in love is always present in the depths of their beings, who yearn greatly to return to this beautiful and loving reality.

A reality that was lost through planetary exiles, where through constant insistence on the paths of pain, we lost the light of our bodies and fell in vibration to a denser place, where harsher laws reigned. Through this fall, it is necessary, in due course, to return to evolution and the paths of love. For it is nothing more than a learning experience, so that souls can once again understand that only the paths of love are the way to constant happiness. Without first understanding this, we won't be able to access this distant dream of paradise that we know so well in this world through religions.

No suffering is eternal, and there is no such thing as endless punishment. There is no such thing as a "*sin*", or rather, a mistake without forgiveness. We are bombarded with situations, words, people, presences, spirits and statements that lead us to believe that there is no way back home. If only they knew that when they stop running from their actions and seek love for their souls, they will be amply supported and helped by the light. And there, they will understand that for everything there is forgiveness, for everything there is rest from the pain suffered, and for everything there are infinite ways to live in peace, harmony and endless prosperity. Never through pain, but only through the awakening of love and the growth and evolution of their beings.

Because everything evolves and everything moves in this universe. If you stop to think about it, nothing is standing still on this earth. Everything moves, everything has its form, everything has its flow and everything has its vibration. Through it, everything around you takes shape according to what the heart emanates, whether it's realities of love, peace and abundance, or difficulties, problems and constant negativity. I realize that anger, rage and separation are very present in this world. Vibration attracts vibration, and as long as we don't change ourselves, we won't be able to change the field around us. If we insist on pain, it will insist on us. But if we insist on love, it will surely insist on us in full divine abundance.

Perhaps that's why something indescribable like love will always be the key to everything. Only by feeling can we understand and see with our own eyes that love is always what elevates us, what makes us better, what makes us wise and compassionate. Love is always the beginning and the ending point, the road traveled and the goal to be reached. For all pain is fleeting, but love is always eternal.

The Beatitudes are manifesting themselves in this world once again, in a different way, but with the same vibrational content. With the same light and the same energy, to bring their love to wounded hearts longing for a spiritual balm. I realize that these beatitudes bring us a path to uplift ourselves and get to know ourselves in a completely different way that we have never before had the opportunity to understand and feel. Bringing revelations to our lives, showing the hidden in our paths, raising our minds to contemplate perfect worlds of light. And making us understand that, through light, everything is possible.

Yeshua - ישוע

In perfect love, in a will so great that it burned in his chest, the being we know as Yeshua accepted the mission of coming to this world and answering the cries of lost souls in ordeals of the life. These souls were looking to heaven for support to end their earthly pain. Their cries reached the ears of the beings of light; however, the law of severity and punishment still reigned in this world. And without the light of knowledge, they were doomed to learn through their mistakes, due to the great personal and collective karmas that humanity possessed. Unless they somehow, chose to pass through this life more peacefully, choosing to learn from the embodied avatars and souls who left their evolutionary messages to their societies while alive.

When Christ came to this world, bringing a new word based on love, an old pillar was duly broken, an old law abolished. And the Earth was reborn for a new, brighter time in this world.

Once again, what can we say about Christ? We must only feel, feel his essence, because by feeling we can know him. Just seeing is not enough, because our eyes can deceive us with fleeting images. Hearing is sometimes not so powerful, unless those words are bathed in love and truth. Then a change and a part of Jesus' energy can be felt. Jesus Christ, of such deep and true love, whose words touch the hearts of those who hear him, who changes the paths of those who seek him. Whose light is so beautifully felt, who lifts us up, supports us and loves us without judgment. Without the famous "but". Because in love, there is no sin, only acceptance and the deepest, most fraternal love.

Now, I can describe that, in its deepest meaning, Christ represents the love that welcomes, the love that supports, the love that takes your pains, the love that raises you up, just love. My contact with this golden Christ energy has taught me many things about him, experiences lived in love that can only be told in this way. During this time, I was able to perceive aspects of Yeshua that are hidden from the eyes of humanity. Because of the society we live in, it is natural to separate rather than unite, as the system we live in is exactly designed for this purpose. We live in a matrix, in fantasy realities instead of the touch of the earth on our feet, the feel of nature in our daily lives. Contrary to what this world preaches, we are not separate from nature, but part of it.

Who hasn't felt a sense of renewal after a swim in the sea or a walk in the woods? In perfect worlds, this is the common reality of evolved spirits. Where jungles of stones and concretes give way to countless flowers, trees and green fields in a vision of such profound beauty. One example is the planet Venus, where the sky and seas are purple, with advanced architecture in harmony with the earth. In this world, I perceive Christic energy as an energetic form, a vibrational canvas or a perfect geometry. A heightened sensation, a breath of life, a stunning happiness, a life in completeness. Something, someone, a force, a being, an energy so subtle and powerful, an infinity. Visions of stars and constellations hover over my mind at this moment, a radiant star, a light that longs to shine and illuminate all the dark particles, to shine the sacred universe with this endless light. To turn everything into light, to turn everything into this deep and sacred light, to become and only to be, to be light.

We can learn a little about Jesus' personality during his brief time in this world. He enjoyed the company of his apostles, but needed his time alone to recharge. He could love and be loved, living to fulfill his mission on Earth. In addition, he absorbed the ways of the Jewish people during his lifetime - after all, he was born, lived and died as a Jew. As I write these words, I perceive beams and orbs of golden light around me, sensing the presence of Christ. As you read these words, feel this energy and sun-like presence enveloping you right now.

Despite the various titles, nomenclatures and forms that we can see in this man, I have learned that the best way to experience this brotherhood is by recognizing him as a humble brother. On the higher planes of existence, there is no such thing as greater or lesser, titles that place people on thrones and commands to be obeyed, or spiritual forms so great that they cannot be accessed. In the light, we are all brothers and sisters, contributing our due positions for the greater good of all, always with a lot of light, charity and love among all.

The symbolism of greater and lesser is deeply rooted in our society. And it is still part of the denser, darker planes of our world. I emphasize that, in the light, we are all brothers and sisters. If we look at light as a goal to be achieved, and contemplate a spirit of light, we see their evolution as an inspiration to become better every day. Not as envy or diminishment of ourselves in our current state, but only as an inspiration and goal to be achieved. After all, who doesn't want to evolve? And reach a longed-for state of purity and enlightenment like the great masters and avatars of this world? Who doesn't long to be great in truth? Who doesn't long to be one with the universe? And to feel so naturally its movements in our bodies, and just to be one with the Father.

I write these words because I constantly perceive movements of darkness that often try to place greater and lesser in spirituality. Between king and servant, commander and the one who carries out the orders. With great effort, they reflect the dense realities that reside on the lower and dark planes of the light, and often like to compare spirits in order to diminish one from the other. For example, one spirit has more light or brilliance than another, such a spirit has more light or brilliance than you or that a certain person is more evolved than us or vice versa. When you feel this kind of thinking that separates and diminishes someone instead of uniting, evolving, loving, welcoming, shining, realize that it's just a negative movement aimed at separation instead of union. Prayers at this time are so effective that they instantly stop the reverberation of this energy and cease the actions of the being who emanated it.

I know it can be difficult for many people to read these words, to read about a Christ of love, acceptance, purity, elevation, without judgment, pain, prejudice, without negative attitudes or words, without prophets at their command, without anything that could hurt you in any way. For if you have hurt, diminished, denied and offended in any way. It was not come from the light. And it didn't come from Christ. Even those sweet words around poisons and judgments. Using good to justify evil. Using light to poison a person or a situation with words of darkness. The misrepresentation of the essence of Christ is unfortunately very common today. And practiced by many people who follow a word, but don't feel in their essence what comes from unconditional love and what comes from the inverse plane of the light.

Even though I know that the Christ you experienced in your lives was something totally painful, traumatic and bad. But first of all, I want to ask you all a question: was it the energy of love manifesting in your life? The energy of welcome, fraternity, peace, security, non-judgment, upliftment and vibrational strength that only improved your life and made you a better person? If not, I'm sorry to tell you that what you are suffering from did not come from the Christ energy and did not come from a being of light. Even before those who shepherd multitudes of people, but in their words only preach hatred, discrimination, intolerance in all its forms and the subjugation of peoples, verily I say to you, they only serve the lords of darkness. For learn, in love, there is no sin, there is no error, there are no ways and means to diminish you as a human being or as a spirit in truth. There is no welcoming with an air of judgment, nor is there the chanting of loving and painful verses at the same time. I ask you all to take some time out of your lives right now and analyze those who were behind all the pain you have been through in Jesus' name. Will you see love? Or will you see strange, dark forms, or luminous forms with deformed human aspects, and above all, with their dark, dirty and stained interiors? For this is the reality of spirits who falsely emanate light. They are like luminous shells that only deceive the eye, but inside they are rotten with vibrations and illusions that are in fact hellish.

I ask you to always carry out this exercise in your lives, not just to understand your past, but for everything that comes your way. Ask yourself: does this come from the light? Is this from unconditional love? Is this elevating me in love, making me a better person in serene and peaceful ways? Or am I being punished with words and promises for my greater good through pain, karma, God's laws, punishments and the supposed mistakes of the past? Does the Divine Creator really want me to suffer? Does the source of eternal life really want me to go through pain, with the path of love, hope and perseverance as my way up? If it has caused pain, discomfort, if it has diminished you, if it has tried to erase your existence, if it has gone against your deepest being, it has not come from Christ. Always be wary, because in the true Christ, only love and light are present.

Taking homosexuality as a simple example. Many people are diminished for being LGBTIAPN+. And they spend their lives, especially in childhood and teenage years, with traumas generated through guilt, sin, fear of hell, the feeling of having to please their family in order to be accepted, etc. Exercising the previous teaching, did these situations really come from Christ? Were they connected to the energy of unconditional love and acceptance without judgment? Or can we see those dark shapes we talked about earlier? People would be surprised to know the extent to which entities in the form of goats control large churches from behind dark, negative thrones.

I'm going to tell you about an experience I had some time ago. My uncle and I were walking through the streets looking for a heating resistor for a shower that had burnt out at my aunts' house. On the way to the warehouse, there was a very beautiful church outside, big and looking like it had a lot of worshipers inside. At just a glance inside, I could see a dark throne in the middle of the platform or altar, where the word of God is preached. Historically, the symbolism and strength of thrones are a sign of royalty, power, prosperity, command, strength and authority. Many spirits from the opposite plane to the light wish to grow in their negative societies in order to sit on a throne, just as, while alive, they were subjugated by kings and queens on their thrones around the world. The subjugated will one day want to subjugate too.

The throne I saw emanated an energy similar to black smoke and fire, with very dark and opaque brownish tones. It had shades of red, and there sat the true commander, or rather, a commanding servant of someone greater, for the control of all the people who sought shelter and help there. The throne was not visible to the naked eye, only those with open spiritual vision could see it.

Due to these dark thrones and the presence of spirits who wear black, dark hats, who walk the depths of hell in search of slaves, subjugating sick and suffering spirits. Seeking more and more population control, this is why many people turn away from Jesus and the light. Because of the influence of these spirits, who have many forms, clothes, ethnicities, colors, etc. They manipulate words, mislead, command armies to fight the light and spend their existences there in darkness, running away from their own consciences and mistakes, afraid of being caught and punished by those they have hurt, by their superiors and by every negative command that exists under our soil.

Inside the Earth, on the spiritual planes, they hide in caves, cities, palaces, castles, brothels, slums, laboratories and from there they command all their negative plans against humanity and the light. Little do they know that love and light are also here for them. And in the luminous houses of the astral realm, they are lovingly welcomed, supported and cared for with great love and respect. There, in the light, they will not be flogged, persecuted, punished, enslaved, judged, destroyed, killed or forced into exile. Only their own consciences will be enlightened and they will be able to live in peace in the harmony of Christ.

One thing I have learned in my contacts with the blessed angels, with the presence of the beloved Archangel Michael and the loving mentors, is that there is no separation between the beliefs and religions of this world on the spiritual plane. As life evolves in this world, as the Earth ascends to more subtle vibratory realms, humanity begins to connect with its Divine Self and with the Creator. Where the presence of religions, gods and forms of deities is no longer necessary to fulfill this need to connect with God. Because when you vibrate in love, God is naturally present in that place.

The vision of God for spirituality is always the same as what I have experienced and seen with my own eyes: a creative source, an energy, a being so great and so loving that, out of infinite goodness, it is all light, it is all love, it is all glory, it is all beauty, it is all peace, it is all the divine qualities encompassed in a single being. You can feel God in the higher planes, you can contact God in these worlds. We can go to Him, feel this great flash of golden light.

An experience I've seen more than once, when a spirit went to God, all he saw was a flash of light, sometimes a blue so serene, sometimes a gold so bright. Formless, but at the same time with the shape of love. I always see the same image in my vision when the spirits of light speak of God. Such a great energy passes like a sweet breeze through their bodies; everyone closes their eyes and just enjoys this sensation that takes over their spirits at this moment. A faint yet great light illuminates them. God is to feel this strength, this infinite love, this great beauty and infinite goodness and mercy.

It's funny that everyone speaks very highly of God, everyone rejoices in talking about him, everyone can feel him. Like a child's joy overtaking a child, the same joy hangs over young and old alike. Like children receiving a gift from a mother or father, everyone rejoices in talking about and feeling God. We all return to our childhood and become children, pure in the eyes of the Creator, who with infinite goodness welcomes us with open arms at all times.

I like to say that it doesn't matter our mistakes, our failures; for God, these are so fleeting that he's just waiting for us to come back to him. When we take the first step, He walks the first path to us. We understand that everything is provided as a way of learning and evolving our being, and now that you have this knowledge, always choose to tread, evolve and walk the paths of light.

Since Christ is a beloved being of light, it is natural that those who sympathize with him, with his story and with his overcoming, feel naturally drawn to him energetically. Deep down, they want to know this love that is so preached to them here on Earth. As I said earlier, we see Jesus as a brother and a being of light. And for this reason, some works and visions of planetary hierarchies see him as a planetary ruler, a form of vision passed down in Theosophy and the Great Universal White Brotherhood. An egregore of light associated with the white color of peace and the white flame of spiritual Ascension. After all, white is the symbolism of purity, peace and elevation.

Some of you must possess the association of the divine trinity; Father, Son and Holy Spirit. Orthodox Catholic vision of God in three forms. The Word who became flesh to save humanity. Approached from a spiritual point of view, we see certain similarities in this vision and what spirituality brings to our paths. Since God is the source of eternal life, He is the primary factor in the existence of all cosmoses and universes. Naturally, God becomes us, and we are God. To say that Jesus is God is not wrong, but it doesn't exactly fit the vision I want to convey by removing the veils of religiosity from him.

In theosophy, we have a hierarchical system where we see Jesus and various other ascended masters who rule the planet and assist in the evolutionary journey of this world. Although we sometimes see Christ as a teacher of the world and sometimes Lord of the world, not greater or lesser, but a light that shines to reach everyone. In this conception of Jesus, we see him as an Ascended Master of the creator's sixth divine ray, known as the Ruby Ray, where a loving Master rules under the name of Nada.

But I can say with certainty that Jesus Christ is all the light, strength and power that manifests itself in this world. And without a doubt, he is the great prince and planetary ruler of this world.

There are even channelings that show that Nada was Mary Magdalene, a follower of Jesus in her shared life alongside him. We often see Jesus' broken heart in red flames or in paintings of his red robes. They secretly manifest this symbolism of the Ruby Ray. Nada, like Christ, possesses the energies of the Ruby ray in their representations. In my work *"Angelic Magic"*, I described a channeling feeling a ruby fire on my chest, bringing to words a little of this transcribed energy:

"The Ruby Ray is the flame that radiates its energies of love, devotion and unity to the entire planet. This flame represents the fervor of love, passion and the supreme strength of a broken heart in search of growth. Having these qualities, it is inclined towards love, repentance and always seeks to help its fellow human beings. This flame represents a new life free from the mistakes of the past. Its spirits represent the willingness to care for, love and advise all those who seek it. It is the overcoming of all errors and all disharmonies; it is the divine force that moves a being towards elevation. In itself, this flame represents all of this in perfection. And everyone who reads this message will be able to feel the divine ruby rose sprouting in their hearts. And the beloved Nada, with the Lord Jesus, enveloping you at this moment with her radiations of divine love and devotion." - Ars Aurora.

When we come to know this force, this great love, we realize that what we once felt disappears, and this deep love takes over our being. Well, to govern a planet and have this capacity for diligence, wisdom and evolution, you need to have love in your heart. I remember hearing Spiritist accounts saying that Jesus also held the position of ruler in five other planetary spheres; however, this information is not as clear to me as it used to be. I only put it here to illustrate that Yeshua has a high level of evolution, possessed of this Christic energy of unconditional love, and goes about bringing love wherever he goes. He heals all wounds, illuminates all wounded hearts and brings light where there is darkness. Make no mistake, dear brothers and sisters, the universe is always moving towards evolution and never backwards. It is only natural that everyone, at some point in our lives, will possess the light and bring light to all the worlds throughout this infinite universe.

The Kingdom of God

What will be the fate of the Earth under the rule of love? Only endless happiness and joy. This is the reality of all the higher worlds, considered by Spiritist terms to be happy or perfect. Where evil does not exist, where everyone lives in harmony and exercises their innermost abilities and natural talents for the world. These are solar worlds, bathed in love, warmed by the light of the central sun, where fogs, storms and cold times no longer have a place.

Here, love is always present, and there is no more separation of religions and carnal and spiritual wars to afflict their humanity. The only true religion is simply love. There are no gods, entities or beings to be worshiped and no stories that separate rather than unite. From these worlds, so far away and yet so present, the fruits of knowledge and wisdom are harvested and nourished. Understanding that we are all potential Gods, capable of creating our reality according to our vibration to the universe.

We understand that, only in some cases, we experience a life on the physical plane, but without the separation of spirit from God. We understand the difference between right and wrong, we understand our Divine Self, a word very well used in your world today. (At this point, the light guide points out that we as humanity are correctly using the term Divine Self. To connote God at work in our highest version of ourselves). We don't need hard lessons or to walk the paths of pain, because love is always knocking on our door, holding our hands and lifting us higher and higher.

Have you ever thought of a utopia? A world where everyone has everything, and there is no more hunger, thirst, deprivation of basic needs, and everyone lives their days happily? This is the reality brought by the light to the worlds that welcome it. Christ works every day so that this can manifest on this Earth, together with myriads and myriads of blessed spirits, many known and forgotten Gods acting in unconditional and fraternal love. Avatars bringing their lights to this world, who are ultimately brothers and sisters of light, in clothes to suit each person's level of consciousness. Where, naturally, the spirits of light will present themselves in the best possible way, in the most understanding way, for each person in their particular beliefs and patterns of faith.

We remember that light does not separate, it unites. Light loves and does not hurt. Love magnifies and does not harm. We disassociate the Kingdom of God from religion and put it in its rightful place: equality, brotherhood, peace, love, paradise and evolution for all, without distinction of creed, ethnicity, skin color, sexual orientation, and all the countless denominations created by human beings to categorize each other, instead of just loving each essence as it is.

I believe that we can now understand that the planetary regency of a being linked to a belief does not mean the reign of any one religion over the others. Yeshua is not coming to bring the reign of any clergy, but only to bring love and the ascension of the souls that reside here. Unfortunately, this is something I need to say in harsher words, because the misconception of who Yeshua really is still resides in many hearts in this world. But I ask you to be at peace, because the new Earth will have no room for anything that doesn't come from the core of unconditional love.

In a kingdom of love, there is no pain. Only love lives, only light shines, only brotherhood and devotion to its divine self's. I believe that this world is close to being realized. I've already had an experience about the future that I'll never forget. Once, as a child, I had a very realistic dream. At the time, I didn't understand what it was, but I knew it was something spiritual. Today I understand that it was an astral projection.

I was in a school and I was taking tests there. All around me, various spirits were doing their homework to prove that they could carry out their incarnations. I saw myself in a small hall with long wooden benches, similar to those we see in Catholic churches. There,

I saw a spirit who automatically reminded me of myself as an adult. I tried to reach out to him, but I couldn't seem to do it, and I realized that he was a spiritual brother who was doing the work there.

Many years later, as an adult, I found myself there again. This time, I was helping the spirits in their trials, and I had the same experience again, only in reverse. In my adult vision, I saw myself as a child in that small hall of wooden benches, running the same way I saw myself running as a child. It was unique how, in a mixture of reality and fantasy, conceptions of time travel and glimpses of the future were present in that place. Everything seemed to enrich this spiritual experience.

I know that it wasn't really me as a child and me as an adult. But history repeated itself, and the guide of light was there to help me as a way of connecting my past to my present. In one of these rooms, I spoke to spirits who were about to incarnate about the technologies of the time, such as computers and cell phones. I showed them all how a cell phone worked in my hand, and they were all delighted. I talked about the COVID-19 vaccine, a disease that was plaguing the world today and for which there was already a cure. On the other side of the room, a beloved sister dressed in space clothes came from a world so beautiful and pure, the future Earth. From where she said that in the future there would already be vaccines for the human character. I was truly enchanted by the advance of technology, which, it seems to me, will work to correct human DNA to a perfect state.

In the same room, we had a mixture of past and future, with the present connecting the two timelines. Ancient technologies in the eyes of the space sister, and at the same time, up-to-date for me living in this world right now. It's funny and so fascinating how spirituality can so easily connect the timelines in one place. Something so fluid that it becomes common to spiritual mentors and spirits who possess light.

Later on in this experience, I was instructing a spirit who was about to incarnate, and I have never forgotten how pure, joyful and eager I was to have another life on Earth. Once again, I seemed to be talking to myself before I was born: *"Focus on the angels as soon as possible"*. And the brother would smile and go. That feeling is still engraved in my soul, the images I saw, spirits already aligning themselves with their frequencies and professions before they were even born. One who accompanied me was already going to a kind of police station, he's going to be a policeman in his young/adult phase. The same teacher I saw in the exam rooms is present here, happy to be able to share this happiness with you.

"Love yourself, be love, there's nothing else. I've lived through it, I've been through it all, and I've learned that only love matters (referring to the pains of the flesh and life's experiences)". - A guide.

I also remember that, in one of these exams, we had an impossible time recording the questions on the blackboard and answering them on our test papers. A wise test given by the instructor: if alone we can't memorize everything, together as a whole we can help each other write down the questions and answer them. Exercising unity even before incarnation, something necessary for us to be able to live and go through life's trials more easily. It was an experience I will never forget and one that resonates in my life to this day.

Everything, no matter how chaotic, seems to be moving towards love. Even as I write these words right now, I still feel that euphoria, that sensation that passes through my body. A feeling of life, of yearning for life, something indescribable. It seems to me to be an unshakeable desire, something that cannot be put into words. Truly, this experience, this dream, this astral projection, will remain forever in my life. And I will never forget the beauty that I saw in this dream, which was so simple, but at the same time so enriching.

The Beatitudes

Perhaps one of the most remembered passages in spiritism. Christ's Beatitudes are sermons that bring us healing and help us to walk the right path. They are promises made by Christ to those who suffer pain and persecution, where in these difficulties, it is revealed that they will have consolation and eternal rest for their souls. In uttering them, he removes the burdens of conscience, promotes healing and liberation from our pain. It brings the comfort of the Creator's arms and gives the light of wisdom to reveal hidden things that precede our knowledge, to free us from what once hurt us.

In a process of channeling, he received the light into his body and expanded that light to everyone around him. The people of the time didn't have the knowledge you were given at the time. The world was always very simple, and natural causes were attributed to the wrath of God. Every tear shed was the cause of heaven's displeasure. We didn't have the knowledge we have today. People walked blindly through their lives without understanding what was going on in their paths.

Knowing this, Yeshua understood that he could not go against the forces of that place. For his mission was already too difficult, awakening the souls trapped in those old laws of praise and punishment. That's why he spoke in parables, urging people to draw their own conclusions from what he said. His teachings were always shrouded in these mysterious ways through his wise and true words. In his mysteries lay the key to awakening souls from their deep sleep.

What, in fact, are the Beatitudes? Words of healing and personal ascension. Each beatitude works on one aspect of the lives of those who utter it. Fueled by faith and Christic energy, which is increasingly present in the eyes of humanity, it spreads to Earth in an effort to heal, enlighten and ascend every creature. The nine beatitudes can be summarized as follows:

01.° The Prosperity of the Soul.

The Beatitude that teaches us about the treasures of the heavens. And how souls can gather the most beautiful treasures in the house of the celestial Father. This beatitude is linked to the prosperity of the soul, where the greatest of riches and the most valuable of treasures can be found.

02.° The Sweet Consolation of Mary.

The beatitude that brings us consolation for our tears. Bringing us hope for better days, supporting suffering souls and putting an end to their pain. The second beatitude is linked to the consolation of heaven. And in it we can find the wiping away of our tears and the ending of our pain on our journey. It is as if we received Mary's sweet embrace, and in the lap of the eternal mother, we are consoled and delivered from all evil.

03.° The Inheritance of the New Earth.

The beatitude that brings the manifestation of love and gentleness, a quality of all spirits of light and goodness. By practicing this beatitude, it tempers our spirit so that we can naturally be kind and charitable to ourselves and to others. It increases the light of our consciousness; it raises us to more subtle and luminous feelings. Which, of course, can help in treatments against anger, rage, wrath, desires for revenge and all the energies of the matrix and the dimensions below the planes of light. This beatitude brings the inheritance of the new Earth. For only spirits who can achieve states of love will be able to live in a subtler, happier world.

04.° The Arrival of Divine Justice.

The beatitude associated with the Lord's divine justice. This word brings the energies that act on the highest and most perfect justice, bringing balance between man's temperaments and his essence. It teaches and reveals what is right and wrong, showing the middle way to the perfect balance between man's actions and heaven. It protects against all kinds of evil in the face of the trials of the body and the soul. It delivers from all oppressions and teaches how to live correctly in the ways of the Lord. Closely linked to the heavenly courts and the qualities of divine justice, also connected to the influences of Jupiter, the Archangel Tzadkiel and all the beings who hold the scales of justice in their hands.

05.° The Expansion of Mercy.

The beatitude that promotes sweet mercy on our paths. It makes us understand the mistakes of the past and how we can find peace within ourselves in the face of old sins. It expands the energies of love in everything it touches, is one of the most powerful planetary healing tools in existence. This beatitude is connected to the angel Mihael, the angel of mercy and divine goodness. It is a great healing tool capable of working great miracles in a troubled existence that is not connected to the Creator's ways.

06.° The Return to God.

The Beatitude capable of cleansing our existence of all the shells and densified energies that prevent us from accessing the Creator. It helps in the processes of healing and deep cleansing, as well as revealing the reason for our fall; it can also show us how we can find God within us in the purest and most beautiful way. It cleanses our hearts of all sorrows and expands the energies of love and light in our bodies. This beatitude brings us the proper revelations of all that is harmful to our soul and how we can remove these negative influences from our life.

07.° The Pacification of Peoples.

The Beatitude that is capable of spreading peace on Earth. Its crystalline white energies transmute our soul, providing a quantum leap by accessing new levels of the higher planes of light. This word spreads luminosity around the world and touches the depths of beings, whether they are living people or spirits on the spiritual realms. It is the word of the missionaries of light, whose mission is to spread love and increase the coefficient of light on this planet. It promotes peace and the union of all nations under a single banner of unconditional love and union with the Creator.

08.° The Kingdom of God and the Liberation of the Soul.

The Beatitude that reveals to us the reasons for the persecutions of the world and how we can free our souls from them. It brings liberation from those who walk in steps shrouded in shadow and poisons. It creates a protective shield that repels the calamities of anger, discord and injustice. Just as it silences in love the revolts of those who, controlled by darkness, act in profound ignorance of their actions. This word teaches us that everything has a reason for happening in our lives, and shows the true roots of all the evils in our world. It goes hand in hand with the last beatitude, because they come from the same vibratory principle that was spoken in ancient times by the words of Jesus.

09.° The Revelation of Life.

The eighth and ninth beatitudes are intertwined in the energies of revelations and deliverances. It is the beatitude that can reveal your mission in the world, and how you can expand the divine light of Christ on this planet. It also shows you how to expand your own light to every corner of this Earth. Through your life mission, you can understand your purpose in this world and fulfill your spiritual missions that you came here to accomplish. It reveals your divine source and can show you the reasons for your pain, just like your predecessor, providing soul liberation and connection with the divine Creator.

Nine beatitudes which, if applied correctly, can bring about profound changes in our lives. Revelations, changes of path, the enhancement of the soul through the paths of love, peace and mercy. As well as tuning in more and more to the Christic energy of the Creator. By vibrating at this frequency, our paths are taken to purer, more serene and peaceful states. Our essence changes, and we change when we stop living for the world and start living to realize our divine mission on this Earth.

Every soul comes to this Earth with a mission, whether it be learning, repentance, restitution, evolution, awakening, living in order to experience things, gaining discipline, faith and courage. Even, in the case of everyone born with a more enhanced psychic ability, they came to this world to be a link and a bridge between heaven and earth. Each person has their own personal mission aimed at personal learning and evolution, both for the planet and for their own being. There are no greater or lesser missions; they are all valid and always bring what the soul needs to experience at that moment. There are no missions in which people are born only to suffer, because God's mercy and love are for everyone. Even those who embody through dark planes of existence can acquire light and evolve through love. Since love is the most beautiful thing we can experience, living for love becomes the most beautiful life experience, and as Master Nada of the Ruby Ray says, there is nothing exists apart from love.

So, dear brothers and sisters, don't forget that there is always hope for better days and for a better life. For your paths to be changed and for you to live for fraternal and unconditional love. Regardless of your past or the mistakes you have made. For in the light, there is no judgment. The light does not condemn, it teaches us to be better every day. And it tells us how we can make amends for our past mistakes. The light loves, and does not remove you from her fraternal arms. There is no separation in the light.

There is no constant feeling that something is missing or wrong. To be in the light is to be complete. It's feeling that finally, after much suffering, we can live happily and be sure that better paths await us. The sensation of emptiness, discontent, inertia, apathy and the feeling of doom, that there is nothing more to be done or that our paths have been set with no turning back, is completely filled by love. This love makes us feel alive, we can feel life in our bodies, we can once again feel the warmth of love, the sweet touch on our skin, we can feel covered by a light so pure, tenuous and beautiful, and this light simply shows us that nothing exists beyond it. All the darkness of our past and our life dissipates, and we regain the air in our lungs. We breathe after a long period of suffocation and feel the love and life around us, which has always been with us, but now, by taking the first step, we can tune in to feel it in our paths.

I like to speak these words to touch all the hearts that can find themselves feeling cold and distant from the reality. Lost on dark paths, with bad company that only sinks you deeper and deeper into an endless abyss. You, in your innermost being, know what is right and wrong. But the shells created by the constancy of paths not connected to the light prevent you from feeling love in your bodies. These shells are temporary and easily removed if you just choose to feel the light in your lives. I also address these words to all the readers, as well as to all the brothers and sisters who can be found in this temple; there is always a way, there has always been a way, don't let your dark masters deceive you any longer, because there is nothing they can do if you don't allow them to do. Everything is a choice, it has always been a choice from the beginning, and from these choices, we create our reality and live what our consequences present to us on the day of the harvest. Sowing is for everyone. Knowing this, choose love, forget the pain and look upwards, where your help comes from. All you have to do is ask, don't forget that.

With the Beatitudes spoken, new paths begin to appear on the horizon. Yeshua brings new knowledge in these parables, which in wisdom are reflected in the liberations of these individuals' souls. In their worn and harsh realms, the light came to liberate, support and love, never to oppress, diminish or erase their existence. By choosing to go through such trials in life, they all lacked the understanding to choose the paths of love for the sake of their own evolution. The opposite path was so present in their lives, seen with their own eyes on a daily basis, where the severity and wrath of man had no limits and no end. As they witnessed constant punishment and violence in their countless lives, they ended up choosing the same paths that they had experienced over the centuries, and for some, even millennia of time.

Nowadays, there are still spirits from such ancient and distant times who still reside in this world, with such dense energy levels as the actions seen as barbaric in our eyes that were widely practiced in previous times. Due to such density, the light needed to become flesh in life so that a message of love could break the ancient patterns that resided there. The reason for Christ's coming was to rescue the essence of love, to awaken these souls to the light and break the bonds of darkness that sat there on royal and spiritual thrones, where a few coins could be worth more than a life. The pattern needed to be broken so that a new light could appear on the horizon.

When the Word became flesh and came to this world, Yeshua took on the responsibility of changing the thought patterns of many souls who lived here. On a missionary mission of love, his words served to awaken sleeping hearts, reconnecting their souls to their divine essences, thus bringing about an awakening of consciousness. More and more, spreading the words of love and light that have propagated on this Earth. Love has immeasurable power, and by healing the deepest wounds, Christ's words open up a new path for the lives of all those who hear them. Who has never heard an account or testimony of Christ's love saving a life that was on the brink of destruction? The Beatitudes appear once again on this earth to heal through their divine wisdom, awakening souls from their illusory slumber and reconnecting their essences to the divine Creator.

The Revelations

Through Kabbalah, the scriptures conceal hidden meanings given by God to be revealed to mortals. Secrets that, until then, were only available to family lineages or to those hard-working researchers of revelation techniques such as gematria, notarikon, temurah and others. Based on one of these techniques, this book is designed to bring out these hidden meanings in the form of the divine names of each of Christ's beatitudes and open up paths to new understandings, wisdoms and contact with the energies uttered by Yeshua in our lives.

When we access the energies impregnated in the verses through reading and chanting the mantras associated with them, we access the energetic principle that is present in countless forms and ways in this world. I don't want to go into magick formulas and go through the whole traditional process. Today, I want to pass on something simple, accessible and that can be practiced by everyone this book reaches. Including, of course, powerful results for its practitioners.

With the continuous arrival of the Christic energies of unconditional love on this Earth. More and more paths are becoming available for this energy to manifest itself fully in this world. We're talking about this energy accessing everyone who doesn't know about it. In the same way that light wants to illuminate all the darkness of the world at all times, the energy of love also wants to access all those who have not been able to feel it in their lives. This book is a bridge so that all those who don't know Christ can get to know him in a purer way, free from religions or visions already pre-established by humanity. I want to bring this light to wounded hearts that have forgotten the light of love. And in these beatitudes of Jesus lie the keys to inner healing, to receiving revelations of our paths and to anchoring the light and strength of Christ in our lives.

A true mystery is revealed in these pages, and a powerful planetary healing tool is given to each of you at this time. The powerful Golden Star will expand its light in your bodies and illuminate the Earth in this ongoing process of personal and planetary healing and ascension. All the paths are given in these pages so that all of you who read these words can properly awaken and ascend. Just as Christ awakened the crowds earlier in the Sermon on the Mount, you too can receive this awakening as you read on. In these words of light and love, may you all receive Christ's divine blessings in your lives. However difficult your paths may be at the moment, know that no suffering is eternal. And from the revelations contained herein, I know that you will be able to make very good use of the sacred spells presented here.

Still on the subject of revelations, many things have been brought to the surface for humanity in recent times. We've never had so many UFO sightings as we do today. For example, the large number of unidentified objects during the war between Russia and Ukraine. We know that our galactic brothers are keeping a close eye on earthly events. Even though we are still limited to our free will and personal choices, including our personal and planetary karma. Sometimes we can perceive certain interventions from them when something is about to go beyond the limits allowed by spirituality, especially when suffering goes beyond our karmic debts.

So many revelations from ancient times brought to the world today, they are present on all media platforms around the globe. I know that the system's days are counted down to their end, and I know that much is yet to change in this world, always in due time as stipulated by spirituality. As the light advances to the four corners of this world, more things are discovered and more structures are collapsing. These structures are nothing more than the *"walls"* and *"constructions"*, animate or inanimate, of everything that does not serve God in his greater purpose. In its figurative and real sense, houses not strengthened on a firm rock cannot stand when the storm comes.

"Therefore every man, whoever hears these sayings of mine, and does them, I will compare him to a wise man who built his house upon the rock."

"And the rain descended, and the torrents came, and the winds blew, and beat upon that house, and it fell not, for it had been founded upon the rock."

"And every man who hears these sayings of mine, and does not do them, will be compared to a foolish man who built his house upon the sand."

"And the rain descended, and the torrents came, and the winds blew, and beat upon that house, and it fell. And great was the fall of it."

Matthew 7:24-27

Even if the earth shakes, even if the seas rise, even if the winds threaten to blow and carry everything away, every building well-founded on the rock will stand still until the end of time. When the renewal is over, when the old structures no longer exist, the world will be able to see on its horizon a new era emerging, far from the old laws that imprisoned humanity. Now, the Earth is entering its state of regeneration and will finally become fully illuminated in the eyes of the Creator.

I realize that the more we are connected to a good frequency, the more in tune we are with this golden Christic energy, the more lucidly we perceive the things that happen around us. And we receive profound revelations of what controls our world. This control becomes so visible and palpable in our hands that we awaken in such a big way, we actually see the countless forms of population control. The Christ energy comes to increasingly awaken this century from its evils and promote this deep internal cleansing in our bodies. We know that the work of deep cleansing is sometimes complicated for certain individuals, but with the support of spirituality, it becomes light and serene. By choosing to walk the paths of justice, by walking the middle way, where we achieve a balance between our desires and wishes, we will know how to live in harmony with our bodies, our lives, our paths and our destiny in this world. Always knowing that we can choose to walk lighter paths, watered by beautiful flowers from the countryside, where peace reigns, and a sweet breeze carries our hair in a calm summer dance.

When the word is revealed, when light dispels darkness, when love overcomes darkness, when Christ becomes present in the heart of every individual, then we will see the golden age. Where only love will reign and where only the beatitudes of the soul will be part of our daily lives.

Planetary Healing Through

the Golden Star

Every day I realize how urgent it is for humanity to start getting in tune with God and sending light to this planet. It's not uncommon these days for spiritual mentors to ask for prayers for this Earth on an almost daily basis. If I could describe how terrible the consequences of wars and all the evil emanating into the planetary energy field are, I could say that they are like days of astral darkness hanging over the world. As frightening as it sounds, on very dense and dark days, it seems that even the air we breathe becomes toxic. The astral energies become like poison. Quite recently, I could hear something like cries of pain in the winds on a dark and dense night. It wasn't the first time I'd heard such clear and dark auditory events. From time to time, when the Earth is gripped by such darkness, the skies turn black in energy density. Clouds of darkness hang over the world. Winds that echo voices of terror knock on our bedroom windows. In humanity's past, when this Earth witnessed the First and Second World Wars, the same weather was present in our world. Countless cloudy, cold, dark and melancholy days. Something like a weight in the air, a weight on our shoulders. We know then that it's nothing more than the result of darkness gathering over the collective of humanity. The denser it is, the darker the sky gets. On endless cloudy days, we know that something strange is happening outside the ordinary eyes of human civilization.

Seeing to believe. If everyone could see the black flames manifesting in the astral, then they would know that humanity's ways are not right and that we need an immediate change. I've never been a cold person, living in a tropical country, I realize that cloudy, sunless times are an alarm that the Earth needs light. For I know that when the weather turns dark, a great darkness spreads through the streets of this planet. Much of my experience of the current planetary situation has been provided by tuning in to the energy of Reiki. And when I was taken to places that urgently needed light, I realized that these points of conflict in wars, or in natural disasters that promote a large number of deaths, are places with a lot of suffering where the astral field is harmed. This great wound that opens up in the planetary field is similar to a wounded and open light, with opaque and very weak dark blue tones, and an opaque and lifeless faint black.

The great humanitarian catastrophe in Gaza and the never-ending conflict between Hamas and Israel opened a wound in the planetary layer of that place. That wound remains to this day as I write these words. There are still dead soldiers there, thinking they are still alive and firing their weapons at each other. I can give the same example between Russia and Ukraine. And, of course, in all the places where there are frequent wars and deaths around our globe.

The spirits remain in constant suffering in these places. Even decades after these events, there are still wanderers in these places today, where they believe they are alive and relive the suffering of their deaths on a daily basis. The consequences of war don't just occur in places of conflict, but spread across the globe like a noxious and catastrophic wave. Think of it like a poisonous wind that travels from city to city, causing harm and disease, or like intoxicated water that crosses the oceans and reaches people's homes.

Unlike condensed physical matter, which takes a while to reach its proper place, whether that time is quick or long, the energy is instantaneous in every corner of this world. If a collective death occurs, that is, if many people die at the same time in one place, the whole world feels and suffers from all the pain and despair emanating from those people. Now, I ask you to imagine the size of the energies caused by wars and natural disasters. And even silent disasters such as the poisoning of our rivers and seas, the deforestation of nature, the cold and bloodthirsty killing of animals to feed the population, the constant control of dark spirits in churches, palaces, kingdoms, companies, politics and world organizations, where they are constantly opening wounds in the planetary vibratory field.

Everything that is not connected to the light hurts its possessors. And if just one soul is wounded in this world for whatever reason, that wound is felt all over this Earth, whether on a larger or smaller scale. All our actions have always had global and even galactic and universal consequences. Humanity cannot live in peace as long as it carries out actions harmful to God's soul, which are carried out daily by us men and women. When a person is diminished because of their gender, or their social status, ethnicity or their appearance or skin color, naturally that pain will reverberate in some way, bringing more pain, more prejudice, more diminishment. This will cause hatred, anger and, consequently, collapse personal or collective desires for revenge. So many examples could be given here, but I am already aware that the message can be understood by everyone by now.

I've said before that we are not separate from nature, but part of it. Our soul is one with it. If it dies, so do we. If we treat it badly, we also suffer from that mistreatment. Individualism and the separation of the soul of God into the soul of the ego are just ways of opening wounds on our Earth. The dark lords know very well that when a soul chooses the path of ascension. It is connected to a crystalline healing network, where various mentors and luminous spirits take part to help this soul in its awakening and personal growth. In this collective, the soul evolves and ascends. And the dark lords know that the personal journey into darkness is separation from the divine. It is harmful in every way. However, beautiful words, books and poems are used as a way of manipulating the truths of this world in regeneration, in order to get new souls to separate from their divine essences and follow more illusory paths, not connected to the Creator.

I can say that I have already entered certain places where I have been allowed to go, for my own evolution and awakening. And I can say that I have seen the faces of those who hold their thrones and manipulate events for population control. Sometimes, I perceive negative grids and pre-established bases in the Earth's vibrational field, precisely to hurt the energies of the place and reduce the vibrational level of the world, like antennas organized by beings who are not connected to the light. In astral projections, I've even seen the use of machines scattered throughout the streets, forming a dense fog. On the same day that I had these experiences, my state and several places around the country were covered by cloudy weather and a low-vibration energy that hung over the houses.

I felt myself slowing down, just wanting to stay in bed, on one of those foggy days with a strange feeling that reminded me of planetary healing. I decided to do some intercession by getting into the right mindset and start sending healing to this planet. That feeling that was lodged in my chest melted away and I could see the sun rising over the Earth once again. I understood that that depressive feeling, those harmful thoughts and that feeling of tightness were nothing more than planetary density, something extremely common these days. You know that common line when people get sick or more agitated than usual and say that it's the *"moon"* interfering with their emotions? Well, the moon certainly plays a powerful energetic role in our world, so strong that even the seas of the oceans become more agitated during periods of full moon, the moon being associated with the element of water. Naturally, it will influence all these elements in our world. And we human beings are made up of more than 70% water in our bodies.

We can give the same example of energetic influence when nations rise up against each other, collapsing, that is, exploding all the energies that have not been properly worked on and healed over long periods of years. The act of bringing something to the surface in our daily lives is a tool of mercy from spirituality, because in this way, even through pain, we can face up to past problems and resolve them in one way or another. Even though these wars are taking place on these worlds, it is also a form of personal and collective karmic cleansing of nations. Now, all those who have been affected by it in some way, whether actively or not, consciously or unconsciously, also have some past connection with these events that are taking place today.

When we promote a means of collective healing, be it through prayer, meditation, Reiki or other techniques that send light to this planet, we are helping to release the darkness in the planetary collective and within each person. The more light a human being receives, the less aggressive they become. Exactly when we receive prayers, which are forms of light, they calm our spirit and bring us a beautiful and comforting sense of peace. In the same way, when we pray for our problems, they also receive light and are solved much more easily. Conflicts cease to matter, past grudges are forgotten, and the soul is untied from these binding chains in order to experience joy in its current state. Healed, peace takes over our daily lives.

Now, imagine how powerful it would be if everyone reading these words took a few minutes out of their day to say their prayers to the planet. Even less than 10% of the world's population vibrating light to this world already makes a huge difference to the planetary energies. Imagine the whole of humanity vibrating in nothing but love and light. A simple prayer like the Our Father or a Hail Mary directed at this Earth can already have great beneficial effects and help prevent many negative timelines from activating in our reality. Timelines are nothing more than probabilities. If certain events or energies come together, vibrating in a certain tune and pattern, these timelines naturally activate in our society. If humanity decides, from one moment to the next, to vibrate light and love to the planet, giving up its crooked ways and practices once and for all, the world will completely change its vibratory pattern, and more subtle and harmonious timelines will become realities everywhere on this planet.

In the same way, if people, spirits and the collective, for the most part, insist on more negative paths, more destructive timelines will become realities on our globe. In these cases, it is the collective intention of humanity that plays a blind game, where they are unaware of their actions, but just follow a flow of actions and consequences in their lives. Because they are blindfolded, they have neither the knowledge nor the wisdom to understand that their actions, thoughts, desires and intentions can have a global impact. For this reason, they are widely manipulated undercover to think, act and do what the inverse plane of spirituality wants. Perhaps this is why the work of awakening souls is so complicated in this world, because we face the greatest resistance from those who are not awakened to love, who in no way want their plans to be annulled by the light.

Talking a little more about the planet's burden, the density of the Earth manifests itself as a dense dark fog, this darkness that stains the subtle bodies of the planet. The planet also has its spiritual bodies, and these bodies can end up being tainted by the low energies generated by humanity. I remember once seeing the Virgin Mary in a place of light, inside a protective dome or shield. Outside this shield, I saw something like a dark fire, with shades of black, gray and dark blue that burned outside the place. In a spiritual colony, spirits are safe due to the protective measures these spirit cities have in place. However, we people, don't have this protective shield in the cities, making a large part of the population vulnerable to the symptoms of this mass production of feelings not connected to the Creator.

Sometimes it's wise for the world's population not to be able to see what's going on in the more subtle planes of this world without the proper level of understanding and evolution. That would only cause collective chaos. Imagine what this world would be like if all human beings could see each other's aura. Certainly, they would keep a great distance from realizing the real energy of their partners, associates, friends, acquaintances, family, etc. If everyone could see the planetary energy of their homes, the chaos that would ensue would be unprecedented.

Certain psychic gifts are only granted to those who, in maturity, can handle this type of information without getting lost in what these visions can generate. I'm not saying they're special, because every human being can reach this state of clairvoyance. All it takes is for this psychic ability to emerge through practices that are healthy for the spirit, as it is a natural gift present in all of humanity.

That's why the more light this Earth receives, the more subtle the steps of this much-talked-about planetary transition will be. This way, more conscious people will be able to see what's going on under the veil. When we leave a dense world of old conceptions about God, the world and our society and enter a world of light, liberation and connection with our inner selves, we will know how negative our life was in the past and how wonderful our life is living in a heavenly paradise.

As a result, I decided to develop a personal and planetary healing technique, with the help and channeling of my beloved guides, Angels, Archangels and spiritual mentors. A technique called *"The Golden Star"* was born. The Golden Star is a technique first introduced in my book *"The Magic of the 72 Kabbalistic Angels: The Complete Guide to Contacting Heavenly Forces."* In it, I was able to pass on a powerful personal healing technique to devotees of the angels. Instead of just working on personal healing through psalms and connecting with our guardian angel, I decided to expand so that this inner work could be amplified on Earth.

The Golden Star was born as a way of expanding the celestial forces to the world and, at the same time, amplifying the golden energy of Christ so that everyone can receive from this ascension healing energy. The golden energy of Christ is capable of performing true miracles, and I can testify to this through my devotion to St. Michael the Archangel and through Archangel Michael's wonderful 21-day prayer.

In this book, the Golden Star returns, refined and empowered as a way not only to illuminate all the darkness around us, but also to be planetary healing tools by exercising mastery over our lives and expanding that light to the entire globe. If we knew how great and powerful the force channeled for planetary healing is, we would live in full harmony to heal this world at full power. Great in strength and power, we can obtain its incomparable miracles around us and truly be instruments of light and bearers of our collective healing, serving the greater good of this Earth.

To its practitioners, it will be revealed that it is not just based on a meditative or projective technique of magical symbols, sacred geometries or channeling the rays of the Creator. The Golden Star performs a process of inner illumination, merging practitioners with two very powerful rays known to the Great Universal White Brotherhood: the ray of Christ, the golden flame of perfection and completeness, and the Violet flame of Saint Germain, the powerful transmuting and purifying flame, key to the healing of this world.

In the next chapter, I'll talk more about how it works and how, descriptively, the Golden Star can help you expand your light and heal your inner wounds with the help of the sacred Hebrew Pantacles of the Beatitudes contained here. This knowledge was kept hidden for a long time, and only initiatic orders had access to how the Hebrew letters could cause great changes in the human psyche. Being a way of channeling light, the practitioner will increase their energy level and raise their vibratory pattern in the process. By raising their vibratory pattern, they will be able to access the subtler worlds and continue their quest for personal growth and evolution. By accessing God, the practitioner understands that they become God in action, and everything is completed, becoming the palpable truth in their hands.

By enlightening and exercising our mastery over ourselves, we consequently change the world around us. We don't need to save the world, but by saving ourselves, we are already playing a great role in our earthly journey.

The Golden Star works on both of these things. By working on this sacred magic for your life, you will automatically be helping to expand this light to the world. By healing yourself, you heal all the situations around you. In this expansive effect, beautiful changes manifest on your paths that are bathed in this powerful divine light. In the Golden Star, by bathing our bodies in the golden light, we are expanding it to everything around us. By expanding this golden light to planet Earth, you will bathe every spiritual part with this light, which will consequently open more doors and opportunities for spiritual mentors to act on behalf of those who need their nurturing.

By expanding this energy, you can also promote a process of healing and liberation in the umbral zones (also known as hellish zones or zones of suffering). When the light comes, it illuminates troubled minds and dispels the darkness clustered in these underground caverns of our Earth.

The Golden Star has no space or time limitations. You can send it to all the people you want, all the places you need. Wherever the golden light wishes to touch, it can be sent with the great force of unconditional love. The healer can play a great role in sending this energy to areas of great spiritual density, areas of war and conflict, political areas, situations that demand great wisdom, such as elections and local presidential meetings and/or those of the countries of this world. In addition, it can be directed to less developed countries, where people face hunger, lack of basic needs, lack of rights, discrimination and other challenges.

Areas in conflict or which have suffered a natural disaster are the most requested by spirituality to send prayers and light. These prayers are of great value and help at these times. Certainly, many spirits who have passed away can receive the warmth of prayers for their souls, and we, as healers, can we provide great relief from their pain after death, with such a difficult time.

Much of the destructive energy echoing around the planet comes from the countless mass deaths in conflict zones. Another point that is very present are the places that have been destroyed due to natural events, such as earthquakes, tsunamis, hurricanes, storms and fires. These are small examples of the fury of nature resulting from the environmental destruction that this planet suffers on a daily basis due to the greed for profit and the sovereignty of certain individuals over the mass population.

When these things happen, be they wars, mass deaths or natural disasters, a great mass of negative energy is emanated to Earth. This mass is based on feelings of fear, anger, revenge, greed, despair, death and the like. Now, imagine this whole mass being strengthened by thousands of people vibrating to the same tune in these places. Consequently, this energy lodges itself in the Earth's vibrational field, resulting in its partial or complete darkness. When this mass covers the world, the whole vibratory pattern of the Earth drops, which leads to more bad things collapsing and happening in the lives of its citizens. And the more bad things happen, the more negative vibration is emanated. Creating a continuous cycle of negativity and imprisonment in a dense planetary karmic energy wheel.

When a soul breaks this recurrence, in other words, when it awakens and chooses to follow another path that doesn't feed the anger that hangs over the world, it frees its lower and higher consciousness from this endless cycle of hatred and negativity. Automatically, this wheel breaks, and as the awakened being has not vibrated to its negative tune, it no longer reverberates through them. Only one soul can make tremendous planetary changes. Only one being of light can make such a huge change capable of altering the destiny of everyone who lives on this globe.

Now, imagine how powerful it would be if several awakened souls vibrated to a greater tune of unconditional love. These vibrations would certainly not only be felt here, but throughout the universe. No wonder Earth has spirits who have come from all corners of the universe to witness the Planetary Ascension. For the souls of light who live here are seen as warriors who carry the word of love in their lives.

It's also important to mention that we must all play our part in this world and not fall into the comfort zone of leaving all the work to a few. Laziness will certainly not lead us to greater paths, only to contentment with our current reality with no prospect of significant changes.

That's why it's extremely important for the souls who reside here to wake up to their life paths and play their part in healing this planet. You don't need much; every prayer helps. Every form of light is valid. If everyone who reads these pages can take a few minutes out of their day to vibrate for the Earth, I'm sure that wonderful things will happen on their paths. For he who vibrates in love will also receive love in his life. Those who vibrate in healing will be healed. He who vibrates in mercy will receive mercy. And he who vibrates light will also receive light.

The Rise of Vibration

Everything that exists in this universe is made up of energy. Everything is vibration, everything emits a vibratory wave. All animate and inanimate things have their own vibrational frequency, their own *"sound wave"* that vibrates naturally in their day.

We can exemplify vibrations by waves in Hertz, which is a unit of frequency used to diagnose the various forms of waves around the world. Hertz are sound waves that vibrate at a certain frequency. The higher the sound wave, the faster it pulses and travels, and the lower it is, the slower it pulses and travels.

It can be seen that distorted feelings such as shame, guilt or fear are the worst and have the lowest vibration. Apathy, the indifference of not feeling anything about the people and/or situations around us, also reveals a great danger. Even if you're in a more neutral state of appearance, in reality you're vibrating in dark, soul-damaging vibrations. Vibrations so common in entities from the inverse plane of light.

I can testify that the denser the spirit gets, the angrier, more apathetic and brute it becomes. The perispirit, one of our seven spiritual bodies that connects perceptions, sensations and feelings to the physical body, becomes increasingly deformed & monstrous when we choose to go against the divine plan of our Higher Self. A real horror show, where tormented souls take the form of monstrosities that reflect their inner selves and mold themselves to their own wills.

For this reason, entities in the form of goats, dragons, snakes, flies, insects, alligators, lions, and the famous cartoonish demonic forms known to the Brazilian people are common and often used for obscure purposes, such as receiving worship, energy, offerings and controlling their devotees in their wills and desires stipulated by these dark lords.

The form of an animalistic goat mixed with human features is the one most often used by spirits who have people enslaved in the astral world. These, in particular, are very present in Brazil due to the syncretism, religion and magical practices of worship that have numerous strands in our Brazilian soil. On the other hand, the more virtuous our emotions and the higher our vibratory state, the more beautiful, serene and resplendent we become. It is truly a spirit formed of light, where every particle of the being becomes perfect, beautiful, attractive, enlightened and peaceful. And where all feelings are always directed towards love, collectivity and enlightenment.

They say that our interior is a reflection of our exterior. There couldn't be a more absolute truth than that. Our whole world is based on what we vibrate, because everything is vibration, everything is energy, and everything we think manifests instantly on the mental planes of existence. If our thoughts and feelings are good, we will reap sweet fruits on our journey. However, if they are distorted, we will only reap bitter fruit and detours that take us away from our divine essence.

I don't think the common belief that people with serious flaws in their character are showered with luxury and impunity is correct. For if everyone could see the auras and the entities from hell that accompany them, they would think twice about their mistakes. People turn into the worst monsters of their nightmares, and so go about their lives with no light inside. When our beloved mentors, angels and guides ask us to do the famous inner reform, it is precisely to improve ourselves as people and spirits. So that we can acquire light on our path and work on our shortcomings for personal improvement. After all, there is no spiritual evolution without internal improvement and polishing.

As mentioned earlier, our vibratory frequency determines our current state in life. We can use powerful tools to raise our vibrational pattern and shape our reality according to our desires. Mantras are one way of doing this, as are prayers, spells, rituals, sacred symbols, holistic practices, meditations, reiki, energy healing, dowsing and radionics, among others. Everything that raises our standard manifests positive things in our daily lives.

Individuals who are deeply dedicated to their inner improvement, who constantly pray to their faith, always receive support from spirits of light, eliminating the need to use any energetic tool to improve their lives. Their vibration is already high, understanding that they already have everything. By having everything, everything is granted. This is one of the keys to spiritual evolution. Those with higher levels of consciousness and a higher spiritual awakening realize that they have everything they need. In this awareness, all requests are granted, because the light supports and surrounds those who walk by their side.

Unfounded material desires are put aside in this process, they realize that that car, house, motorcycle, job or whatever the flawed projection of the person's EGO feelings is, are just illusions created to mask some internal problem. They won't necessarily bring happiness to the individual. We need to understand that there's nothing wrong with wanting material things, in fact, we should always seek to offer the best for our own being. I've noticed that people have a habit of dedicating themselves to others as much as possible, but when it comes to themselves, they often deny themselves many things, diminishing them in the process. How often do we not give the best to ourselves? This reflects a low-frequency pattern, poor thoughts attract poverty, not only material but also spiritual. The feeling or the energy of lack can manifest itself in various aspects of one's life.

We are asked to always seek a better life. And never be content with the problems and difficulties we face. Seeking higher vibrations and paths more in line with our spiritual mission to bring healing and harmony in all our fields, both material and spiritual.

If what a human being thinks is impregnated in their auric field, attracting to themselves what they have thought, it is natural that our convictions, thoughts and desires manifest what we want. If our mental field is balanced, our aura will be harmonious and will attract harmony to our paths. On the other hand, if our mental field is unbalanced, with small, low thoughts, with vibrations contrary to our being and to our fellow human beings, uttering negative words, judgments, complaints, feeling distorted desires and feeding our most negative parts, consequently, our auric field will be tainted.

Auric fields of this type are often seen as black lights, emanating something akin to black, bluish and gray flames. Red can sometimes be seen with dirty carnal desires, where there is no harmony in their lives. The color opaque dark blue is often associated with sufferers of sadness and depression. Black auras, opaque blue, grayish and sometimes red or with red dots on a black background, indicate great danger. Naturally, people with this type of vibratory field are associated with violent behavior. They are murderers and follow tortuous and dark paths, posing a danger both to themselves and to others.

Make no mistake, brothers and sisters, the path of darkness, malice, revenge, hatred, apathy and impure desires, anything that is not virtuous for the soul, will inevitably lead to an abyss of consciousness. Pain is, in fact, a lesson allowed on this planet. Spirits who choose to walk in the shadows of their consciences will one day be awakened, because they will no longer be able to endure so much suffering for their bad choices. Even if it takes millennia, it is everyone's destiny to walk in the light, because only light exists.

Thus, the universal law applies to everything and everyone. And it is always active. What we emit to the world and the universe is reflected in our lives, whether that emission is conscious or unconscious. Therefore, the process of internal improvement, healing our old wounds, resolving our past issues and establishing harmony with ourselves is of the utmost importance. This search allows us to live happier days and witness more beneficial, abundant and enlightened events during our journey on this Earth.

The Sacred Mantras

Mantras are sacred ways of connecting with the divine, bringing light into the lives of those who chant them. They represent the chanting of light through words that tune into the desired egregore, allowing us to receive this light in our bodies and in our lives. Although mantras are best known in Hinduism and Buddhism, they are not restricted to these divine manifestations in our world and can be expanded to the entire planet. They are a simple and powerful way of connecting the soul to what it seeks intimately. Chanting to God is a mantra, just as repeating positive affirmations and decrees can also be considered a mantra.

The word *"mantra"* in Sanskrit can mean *"mind control tool"* and is used to curb the mental and its uncontrolled thoughts, providing peace and silence to this field. By chanting a mantra, we immerse ourselves in a deep state of meditation, controlling our thoughts and reducing their disharmony in our lives. Mind control is fundamental in the practices of Buddhism and Hinduism, where the mind plays an important role as a means of internal control over the embodied soul. It can be considered a battle between emptiness and enlightenment, emptiness being a non-existent illusion of reality. The soul becomes enlightened by understanding that, living in a world in the flesh and matter, only light exists. All other things are distractions to divert it from its path, including the mind and thoughts that don't contribute with any way, but only take it away from its main focus: living in the present moment and experiencing life in its entirety, in perfect harmony and enlightenment.

From the Gnostic philosophical perspective, we understand that the mind, in its essence, is empty, which is beneficial for the soul. However, the challenge lies in the fact that all thoughts, intuitions, voices, memories, visions, projections and their extensions originate from some external source. In other words, everything that manifests in our mind comes from some spirit, whether it is beneficial, bringing good thoughts, memories, joys, intuitions and paths for the elevation of the soul, or, more often, negative spirits that introduce negative thoughts, inducements, control, pains from the past, culminating in negative states such as depression, anxiety and psychic ailments.

Due to my more open and developed psychic abilities, I can confirm these statements. In fact, everything that arises in the mind comes from external sources and is never internal; the mind is empty and completely manipulable for good or evil.

Mantras, in a Gnostic philosophy, represent powerful forces that act as keys to open doors, allowing the forces of light to enter the devotee's life. This concept is especially evident in Hinduism and Buddhism, where mantras are considered chants, praises and forms of worship. The more beautiful, harmonious and powerful the mantra, the more positive energy is attracted, resulting in various achievements, such as personal evolution, attaining inner peace, guidance, obtaining material goods, promoting changes and revolutions, aiding with healing, among others. It is widely recognized that the power of chants should not be underestimated, because through them many miracles can happen.

We all remember songs and fond memories of a mother, father, grandmother or grandfather singing to us. The old melodies seem to contain a magic that has never been recaptured. We remember their songs and the good energy they bring us. Nowadays, we no longer find emotional melodies that uplift us. We know well that the power of the voice can move mountains, can bring down enemies, can manifest everything we desire. We know that Christ knew how to use his voice when preaching his message, when commanding through his voice and authority and miracles happened. And above all, Christ lived in harmony through the prayers and songs of the psalms to lift himself up at all times.

We chant mantras to bring us the energies of what we seek. The avatars and figures of deities around the world all represent an energetic form, an archetype, a vibrational attunement that attracts and manifests something in our lives. An archetype is nothing more than an energetic pattern that is represented through a figure, image, or abstract or non-abstract concept about something or someone.

The constant repetition of the word love in our lives can turn it into a mantra, attracting its meaning. A single word can be simple but incredibly effective when used wisely. For this reason, mantras are designed to access specific and objective vibratory patterns, consistent with what we are seeking.

When Christ sang songs in his day, he established an intimate connection with God. God was always with him, because Christ was always with God. Throughout his life, in constant prayers, he received the nourishment of his soul, and the angels strengthened him to fulfill his journey. From psalm to psalm, Christ praised God, and God listened to Christ, always reaching out in deep love. God manifested himself there as a man and as a divine being alongside, within and being Christ himself.

What I seek to bring in this work is something similar, a way in which you can chant each sacred word of the beatitude verse and connect with God in this way. It's just another form of connection, a way of connecting with God and altering your normal waking states to a deeper spiritual state, connecting with and feeling the energies and vibrations around you.

There is a secret hidden in these pages, revealed at this very moment as I write these words to you all. There are nine beatitudes presented here, and each one has been assigned a sacred mantra to connect with these blessed words. Each mantra is a divine name that represents the essence of the verse, capable of connecting you with that force and bringing its energies into your life. When used in conjunction with reading and meditating on the desired beatitude, these mantras, separated by syllables, allow each person to intone the sound of each Hebrew letter, conjuring up a sacred mantric magick that sets in motion a vibratory aspect to be manifested in this world.

In harmonious connection, love and mercy are felt in each letter and can bring their energies to those who utter them.

As a powerful force of angelic connections, this book takes us back to ancient times, but not forgotten. In it, a sweet man walked through arid lands, under scorching heat, calm and serene in his essence, fair and strong in his decisions. In his suffering pains, his mission was great, and at the end of his days, he ascended once again to the realms of eternal glory. To this day, he remains there and will remain so for all eternity.

The nine sacred mantras provided in this book are derived from Christ's nine beatitudes. These nine words have deeply touched many people, bringing a profound message to the souls of this world, a message known by all pure and loving hearts.

To chant the mantras, the process is simple. At some point in this book, you will be asked to start chanting these mantras in the most harmonious way possible for you. Don't worry about your linguistic accents or ways of chanting, because each mantra has been separated into syllables, representing each Hebrew letter of the divine name that carries the energy of the verse. The divine name, a hidden name considered by kabbalists who perform decryption techniques on the Torah to be one of the names of God, is chanted and sung to attract the divine presence into our lives, as mentioned above.

I'll give you an example below, then you have the divine name of Christ's first beatitude:

In the sacred seal presented as an example, we have the divine name of the first beatitude. Which can be pronounced as:

אעהכללמה

AhHahKahLahMahHah ou AhAhHahKahLahMahHah

ייחימתם

YehYahChahYehMahTahMah

In this book, all the divine names have been separated syllable by syllable, to make it easier for everyone to understand the subject. And also, to make it easier and more accessible to chant these sacred letters. Including the mantra OM, the key to spiritual awakening and connection with the spiritual planes, and the conjunction of the mystical name of Jesus - Yeshua. When included, this divine name looks like this:

Mantra: OM - Ah – Ah – Hah – Kah – Lah - Mah – Hah – Yeh – Shuh – Ah. OM – Yeh – Yah – Chah – Yeh – Mah – Tah – Mah – Yeh – Shuh – Ah.

For readers and practitioners, simply pronounce the name syllable by syllable separately and you'll get the same effect when you chant the name in *"common"* or *"normal"* sequence as we do in our daily lives.

All mantras must be accompanied by the verse from which they were derived. These verses are chanted daily by countless people around our Earth, carrying with them an energy of strength, faith and hope for all those who seek this energy to heal their inner pain and obtain salvation in their lives through faith. By joining the force of this energy and meditating on the verse, understanding its meaning and what it brings to us, we access a living energy that tells us what we need to hear and understand. The use of the mantra, chanting each Hebrew letter, which in itself is an energy nurtured by Jews and Kabbalists around the world, unites the two forces to manifest our desires and requests to God and Jesus Christ in our reality. I have always believed that the spirituality of different cultures and religions go hand in hand, because there are no conflicts between beings of light. Uniting faith, energy and a magical force, bringing this energy into our lives with a good heart, will only bring us good things and elevate our paths.

When a person dedicates themselves to the path of light, the more the light dedicates itself to that person's path. The opportunity is always there, and taking the first step is crucial for something to happen in our lives. By seeking to walk towards love, light, mercy, passion, salvation, redemption, prosperity, eternal peace and all the beatitudes of the soul, these energies also walk towards us, finding us easily, because with open paths, anything is possible in this world.

I believe that the light manifests itself through many paths and ways to reach all people, regardless of their beliefs and religions. These, at heart, seek to bring comfort, healing and ascension to the souls who reside here, being a way for souls who are unhappy with their paths and actions to find hope and improvement in their existence on Earth. After all, without hope, there is no life, no light and no new dawn.

It is something so profound that it moves the heaviest stone to a new life, far from its hardened past and lacking in springs of love and light. Each mantra presented in this work brings us a little closer to Christ. With each intonation, we are graced with additional revelations, more love and more light. It's a form of magick with the voice, a form of magick with the light. By meditating daily on its symbolism, we attract Christ to us and incorporate his galactic and planetary consciousness into our inner world. With Christ consciousness in action, everything is possible and manifested.

I hope that this information has been clear to all readers and that this form of connection will be put to good use by everyone who has access to this work, taking advantage of these seals, mantras, meditations and activations of the sacred magick contained here.

Daily Practice & The Manifestation

Improving our being, honing ourselves and becoming more evolved versions of ourselves is a daily process, not just limited to one life on Earth. The evolution of a soul takes place over countless lives in the material world and over the eternities of a spirit's existence. Living is an eternal learning process, and we can never claim to have learned everything we need to learn in our lifetime. Such thinking is linked to a flaw in our inferior version, because we limit the infinite adventures and processes of evolution throughout the universe, which certainly have no limits. Eternity is a long period, and it doesn't necessarily have to be full of trials and atonements. Nobody evolves eternally through pain, because evolution requires balance with the lessons of love. These are certainly the most pleasant and desirable for the soul. Covering its entire life, journey and experiences, without the need to suffer in order to learn, restore and evolve.

Daily practice is an essential tool for our evolution, and the daily meditation on these beatitudes and the chanting of these mantras provided here should be incorporated on a daily basis. The techniques taught here don't require a lot of time; in just a few minutes, it's possible to establish a high vibrational standard which, with constancy, can be maintained for long periods of time. The more you practice, the more you connect with the words of the Beloved Christ, the more you feel his love in your being, the greater the sacred support will be and you will feel his high vibrations in your life.

Constancy leads to perfection, and in order to achieve it, we always need to make an effort. We need to move towards our goals, be they material or spiritual. These mantras and techniques presented here will be of great help in your journeys, as they connect to high vibratory levels that integrate your frequency, making the words and feelings of love that were once spoken on this Earth vibrate.

It's impossible to look at Sananda and not feel love. To truly know him in his essence means forgetting about religions and the sayings of men, connecting with his soul, his consciousness and his vibrations entirely focused on love. This is a characteristic of high spirits who have their own light in their multidimensional bodies. I have often witnessed negative spirits being touched by souls so pure that their negative reactions instantly disappear at the touch of love. When darkness meets light, they want nothing more than to remain in that sweet touch that fills eternity. Overflowing with an indescribable sensation that is impossible to express in human words. It is a true cosmic ecstasy.

Imagine feeling the deep touch of love on a soul that, for the moment, has traveled bitter paths. Love envelops, heals, forgives, fills the pain and reaches out for a new path. It brings rejuvenation to the soul, enveloping it completely, without judgment, without pain, without punishment, just love. Sananda, my beloved ones, is a being that everyone should get to know, and I hope that this book can be a gateway to that.

The manifestation of these mantras can occur in different ways, acting on your vibrational frequency and your electromagnetic field, which represents your vibrational field, where everything is manifested and accumulated throughout the day. By changing this vibratory field to something more subtle, harmonious and positive, everything inside and outside you begins to adjust according to your vibration. This is the secret to manifesting your deepest desires in reality.

Although this knowledge is widespread these days, in the past it was kept under lock and key and was the exclusive preserve of kings, queens and high clerics. If the premise that vibration attracts and manifests what we tune into is true, we can use this knowledge to completely transform our lives. Attracting prosperity to our paths, love, evolution, spiritual awakening, internal and external healing, basically anything we can imagine will be granted. The simple practice of vibrating brings to the material world what we emit on the extraphysical planes of our existence.

Our vibratory field sometimes becomes dirty due to the situations, people, practices, thoughts, feelings and distorted desires that surround us, resulting in dirt and astral maggots impregnating this field. These impurities can cause illness, negative feelings, energetic imbalances, aggravated negative thoughts and densities in general. If our field is dirty, we attract things similar to that dirt, making us easy targets for negative entities to act on. Obsessive processes are so common that many people spend their entire lives with some hostile entity by their side. Currently, due to the planetary transition, this situation has worsened, with umbral spirits (negative spirits who inhabit dense regions of the spiritual planes) increasingly present on the Earth's surface. This makes the planetary psychosphere worse, densifies the energies and affects everyone with their distorted vibrations.

Practices aimed at raising your vibration, bringing spiritual protection and promoting an uplifting of your energies are becoming increasingly crucial in the face of these events. Staying uplifted, peaceful and calm is of the utmost importance for getting through these storms and following the path of life in this world. Hence the importance of the Beatitudes of Christ in this work, including the planetary healing techniques with the Golden Star. By applying these forces to ourselves on a daily basis, we acquire their qualities in our persona, change our vibration pattern and enter a brighter path, which can also contribute to planetary healing. As a result, everything in our lives is transformed, as we become new creatures.

Mantras have the ability to illuminate their practitioners, moving luminous energies down to the cellular level. The more brilliance and light an individual possess, the more extraordinary experiences they will have, following one of the most beautiful universal laws, because spirits dedicated to evolution are always blessed by the divine.

By touching the world with the golden light of Christ, you will be helping this Earth to heal from its long-standing pains and wounds committed by humanity during its stay here in this world. How great is a soul who is moving towards personal healing, and in this process of inner healing, is also helping the planet in its global healing? Have you ever stopped to think how great is a spirit committed to its evolution and to expanding its light to its world? The Beatitudes come to uplift, come to heal, come to bring love and mercy to every corner of this Earth. It comes to cease internal pain and heal afflicted souls, it comes to open up a new path in our lives, to heal darkness with light. It comes to make pure and beautiful what has always been beautiful and pure. By removing the illusions of this Earth, humanity will be able to continue its planetary and galactic evolution by moving up the vibrational scale. And finally, find the Creator within itself.

For until now, the Creator is just there. Waiting for us to take the first step, so that he can walk towards us. For some, he has already found them and lives alongside them every day. For others, he is like a light on your right, a warm, friendly touch that is just waiting for you to notice it in your life. In any case, God is always there for everyone. And I know that in due course, everyone will realize this with clarity and love in their hearts. May the Beatitudes bless you infinitely every day. And may only light be present on your paths. In the due love of Christ, I bless you for the light of the Creator in this world.

The Light of Christ on Earth

What does it mean to be light? What does it mean to be a spirit of brightness? Who really is Jesus Christ? And why is he so important in our world? Questions that are debated but little understood. Firstly, forget religion, forget dogma, forget everything you've been taught by man. For none of that will serve you at this time. We're not talking about the figure of Christ and his representation connected to the church movement. We're talking about Christ as a cosmic soul, that came here to help this world free itself from sovereignty, darkness, lies, population control, the famous *"Matrix"* and all its countless energetic and vibrational derivations that connect people to an archaic and dark system. Under the command of people and spirits who want their servants to kneel in order to remain in control.

Would you believe me if I told you that the Beloved Christ is succeeding in freeing this world from everything that binds souls in endless wheels of incarnation? I know that many of you have heard of the wheel of Samsara, the endless cycle that trapped souls go through from incarnation to incarnation, trapped in dense worlds and unable to recover their divine essences. However, we can look at this wheel through different eyes, seeing the process of life as something necessary to polish our essence, and understand that incarnations are not eternal suffering, but necessary pain chosen by the soul as a way of redeeming itself and learning from its past mistakes. If the soul becomes enlightened in this process and learns more subtle paths to follow, it frees itself from the wheel and begins to experience realities that are more in keeping with its vibrational level. Otherwise, the cycle is maintained until all the lessons have to be learnt and healed. In reality, it is not God, nor Buddha, nor Krishna or Shiva, nor the universe, nor our Higher or Lower Self that keeps us stuck in an endless incarnational wheel. It is only ourselves who remain in a cycle of suffering due to our lack of understanding of the paths of truth and love. Nobody puts chains round our necks or binds our feet. No one is forced to incarnate, no soul is pulled by the arm and thrown into a new body that is about to develop. Every incarnation is everyone's own choice. And we shouldn't live it or look at it with disgusted eyes, but learn from every opportunity that life offers us to grow and improve, to correct our faults every day and rejoice in our successes.

You are a spirit of infinite light, and you don't need to live in pain or suffering. You don't have to and you never had to be like that. Sometimes the guilt we carry in our conscience is a way of choosing difficult paths for our evolution. And it is through this choice that we have ended up in a world of trials and atonements. All pain is a choice, whether conscious or unconscious, whether through action or lack of action.

It is very painful for the spirits of light to witness the exile of souls to worlds that lack love. A pain only felt by those whose hearts are as pure as God. To see souls choosing difficult paths, and often being directed to harsher places, because they only harm themselves and their fellow human beings. It hurts those who are pure to see souls who are ignorant of the light persisting on their paths, far from love, unity and enlightenment.

We ask ourselves, why do we persist in our mistakes? Knowing only that our conscience is the one who judges us. For in the light, there is only love, peace and gentleness. Everyone's personal conscience is the judge. But that doesn't mean that there isn't divine justice in heaven. I've been told this countless times by luminous spirits. Everything in our lives is a choice; only what we allow to happen happens. We only do what we want to do. We are what we want to be.

Words of great wisdom, because we remove the blame from others and learn from our own actions. Such was the exile of Capella, where all of humanity came because it couldn't maintain itself in a higher world of love. A true paradise, where there are no systems, bills do pay, health problems or difficulties in our lives. Everything is provided for, because everything moves towards the evolution of the souls who reside there. Where all our time is directed towards activities that bring us pleasure. Activities that bring us joy, peace, happiness, true love and ecstasy. Can you imagine if Earth followed this example? This is not exclusive to the *"paradise"* told by the religions of this world. All the happy planets do it this way. And even in more beautiful, perfect and magnificent ways than humanity could ever dream of. Where everything is provided for the evolution of the being. No chains, no ties, no control, no distractions, no crime, no pain, just light.

Blessed be the Beloved Christ and all the ascended souls who bring this paradise to this world. Where religions cease to exist, and everyone begins to connect with their Higher Selves and with the Divine Creator. And they begin to live together in peace and harmony with all their brothers and sisters on Earth and in the infinite galaxies of this universe. Countries and states cease to exist and there is only one Earth. One earthly people. No separation of borders, colors, ethnicities, no separation of religions, no separation between one and the other. The Earth is recognized as a world of light. And all humanity is considered to be citizens of the Earth and seen by the brotherhood of light in our galaxy.

Sounds like a distant dream, doesn't it? Well, I'm telling you that everything is moving to make it happen. The light of Christ, sometimes seen as an indescribable white. At other times seen as a radiant gold. And perhaps even seen as a powerful Ruby flame. This love, this cosmic consciousness that has come to the world of matter, has caused profound revolutions in this world. Things so profound that they have not yet been revealed to this Earth. Its arrival imprisoned exiled spirits in caves in the lower astral for centuries. For his light was so great that it was impossible for many to remain on the earth's surface.

Ah, if only everyone could meet this beloved spirit of light. Who is as loved on other planets as he is. They would understand his essence in a purer way. And they could connect with their true love.

Yeshua, his name when he incarnated in this unforgettable life. It was truly a great milestone in his own evolution. I know that we need to learn from his essence to be compassionate, calm, serene and peaceful. And at the same time, to know when to act and work on our emotions, such as anger, in the same way that he destroyed the businesses inside the temple of his Most High Father.

Close to us is the Creator. Source of unconditional love, source of tenderness, light, peace, endless harmony. Source of eternal life, source of existence, principle of life, principle of everything that exists. May he be our guide. May light be our hope. May truth be our way. May Christ be our brother. May love be upon us all, in perfect eternity, from everlasting to everlasting, for ever and ever, amen.

Attuning with the Sacred Seals

Each beatitude available here has a Sacred Seal. This seal contains the letters that, in a certain grouping, attune practitioners to the beatitudes. This, as I said earlier, is a kabbalistic practice often used by rabbis. We use a form to access an energy.

The seals of the Beatitudes provided here in this work encompass all the sacred and divine names of the mystical tradition of Judaism known as Kabbalah. In it, we can find all the names associated with God (known as YHVH or Lord), in each sphere of the tree of life. It is a representation of God's creation of our world. The tree of life involves great mysteries and mysticism, with God's work starting from the most subtle planes of existence, until it reaches our physical plane, the most densified (light being densified into physical matter).

According to the eastern esoteric teachings of this sacred order, each sphere of creation is associated with a divine name of God, each sphere (or emanation) is associated with its own name, and each sphere is associated with an Archangel, an angelic choir and finally a planet. In the first divine emanations, instead of having planetary associations, names are inserted that we consider sacred as a way of representing the whole in terms of an association with the divine in relation to the manifestations of matter and spirit here in this universe. The order would be:

Name of God > Name of the Kabbalistic Sphere > Name of the Ruling Archangel > Name of the Angelic Choir > Name of the planet or primordial manifestation. In this version presented to you, we have a sacred complement with powerful divine Archangels not so well known to humanity. And with words of power that exert dominion over the sacred protection and manifestation of God in our lives.

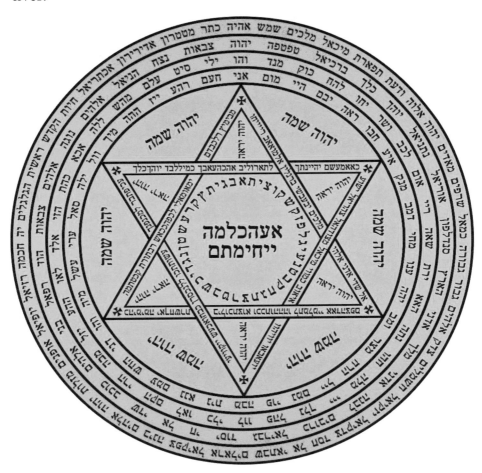

The Seal of the First Beatitude

Starting from the top, we have the name of Eheihe (אהיה). Name of God associated with the Kabbalistic sphere or emanation of Kether (כתר). Followed by the name of Metatron (מטטרון). Archangel associated with this emanation and known as the one who sits next to God the father. We continue with some divine names such as Adiririon (אדירירון). Sacred name of protection in Hebrew magick. Sometimes also known as a very powerful Archangel of God. And Akatriel (אכתריאל), a divine name that is sometimes associated with an Archangel or a form of God related to Justice and the Sacred protection of the creator's presence. In fact, Akatriel to the most sensitive, can see Archangel with a powerful yellow/gold aura with a sacred power in the terms of the Creator's divine Justice.

We have the name of the angelic choir associated with the sphere of Kether (כתר) called Chayot ha Kadosh (חיות הקדש). Which means "choir of living creatures", associated with worship, fire, strength, purity and healing (known here in the West as the Seraphim choir). And lastly, we have the name of the planet, in this case in particular, Kether (כתר) because it is such a subtle emanation, it is not associated with any of the planets in our constellation, therefore, it is associated with the divine name of Rashit Há-Galgalim (הגלגלים ראשית), a divine name that in its mystical meaning represents the movement that gives life to all creation according to esoteric studies.

To exemplify this, the same pattern is repeated throughout the sacred pantacle. Where the names of God, his Archangels, choirs and divine emanations are distributed in a sacred seal that connects its practitioners to the Creator. After the completion of the Kabbalistic Tree of Life, we have the sacred 72 divine names of God, widely known as a powerful tool for meditating with the Creator. Each of the 72 names is presented with a set of three letters, starting with the divine name Vehu (והו) and ending with the divine name of Mum (מום). These names are sources of study, dedication, meditation and spiritual practice around the world, and they are certainly powerful tools that attract and manifest great changes in the lives of people who dedicate themselves to activating the names of God in their lives.

Not only will we find a divine name that is passed on as a mantra or a magic word, but we will also access various angelic names that are included there. And we use them to manifest our will in this world. We have the Hebrew names of all the Archangels, the 72 Kabbalistic angels, all the names of the Tree of Life, angelic choirs and a host of other names to provide and manifest what we desire. Over time, humanity will stop using old energies, and just as it is written, the Lord will make all things new. We always think of this figure as the Divine Creator, father and mother. The divine union of the poles in perfect harmony, where we find only the most beautiful divine gift, unconditional love.

Connecting with these Sacred Seals is quite simple. Just meditate on them for a few moments, observing all the Hebrew letters and names that reside there. Start the process at the name of אהי״ה, at the top of the Sacred Seal, following the subsequent names from right to left until you close the circle at the name of שמש. Repeat the process until you have finalized all the divine names contained in the sacred seal.

We contemplate this divine star, imbued with the golden light of Christ, and we feel its strength and power. We absorb its energy into our spirit. That's tuning in to it, connecting with what it emanates. Many people who are not used to this sacred star feel a strong energetic wave when they look at it, this is common. Meditate for a few moments, feel it and let yourself be carried away by what it brings to you.

Inside the 6-pointed Star, we have the 42-letter circular name of God, which was discovered and decrypted from the powerful Ana BeKo'ach prayer. Its practitioners report countless lights and blessings on their paths. It is an extremely powerful prayer for blessings, protection, strength in difficult times, liberation from all evil, elevation of the soul to the Creator and transmutation of the DNA to a divine state. This is what Kabbalistic belief says, because the names of God act on a cellular level in our organism, restoring divine perfection before the fall at the beginning of time. The circular shape amplifies its center with the names of God. And everything that is written in this way gains strength and power from the Creator. In this way, the powerful Ars Aurora seal is created, which in itself is a perfect sacred symbolism of the Creator's manifestation in this world.

For each beatitude provided here, we have a divine name decrypted from each biblical verse in this work. It is a Kabbalistic faith to seek out the secrets of the Torah and delve into their meanings. For this reason, letters are assigned numerical values, verses are summarized in small words of power, and letters are organized in different ways to discover the hidden things and messages from the Creator that may reside there. This is a widely used way of uncovering new names of God hidden in the Torah. Each central name in all the biblical verses of the Beatitudes contained here represents a hidden name that has been decrypted from the verse and has the representation of the divine name of the verse.

In the past, people connected with this egregore, looking for the seed of creation in their beings. The beginning of everything, the beginning of existence, love in all things. Throughout the ages, humanity has given different names to this. Many faces have been created, imperfect in fact, because in the source of love there are no imperfections. But this does not erase the energy generated, nor the faith that has been placed in it.

We access this energy, in pure heart, to once again bring the light of creation into this world. This is the mission of all the avatars known to humanity. Each one, in a different religious movement, through different aspects, but with similarities between them. We can say that their missions are the same, or at least that they share a similar essence: to bring love and light to every creature. Through their teachings, experiences, mistakes and successes, their stories told, their lives in the flesh, their appearances after death, the mission always refers to the awakening of humanity and the ending of darkness in this world.

Back in Time: The Reception

of the Blessed Words

This is a preparatory technique and, at the same time, a must for us to begin the practices in this book. We'll go back in time to the mountain where Yeshua sat and began to speak wise words to the crowd. We will use this sacred symbolism, the parables not understood at the time, to access his teachings more easily. At the same time, we will cleanse ourselves of the shells that have accumulated in our spirit over the centuries. We will sit in this crowd, listen to their words and receive their energies into our bodies. For some, it could be a transformative meditation, because receiving a deep light in their souls is all they could wish for.

Before you ask, is it possible to access the Beloved Christ in this meditation? Yes. We will access his symbologies and energies spoken at the time. Just as there is no past, present or future, only the NOW. We can go back in time or into the future if we want to. Everything is malleable and can be moulded according to our will.

Set aside a time when you can be alone and quiet, with no noise from neighbors, people in the house, barking dogs or anything else that might disturb the sensory experience you're going to have. On the day you do this practice, keep yourself as calm and pure as possible, without indulging in addictions of any kind, animal-derived foods, sex, violent or traumatic content, etc. Women can easily do this practice during their menstrual periods. Avoid anything that brings a weight or energetic density to your field. The experience will be enriched through your own efforts as you enter into the ancient parables of Christ.

This meditation is an experience of returning to the past, where we access the memories and energies that still reverberate around the world. Much more than just accessing a memory, this practice can be experienced and bring deep revelations as you enter a not-so-distant past.

Before we start the practice, it's important to mention that you should let all the scenes that will be passed on to you in this sacred encounter flow. And above all, read it in its entirety before practicing. I don't recommend stopping to read, as this can break your concentration and experience. You don't need to memorize it either, just let it flow. And get a good idea of what you've learnt in these pages. Read and reread, as this will serve you well from now on.

Having said that, let's get down to business:

01.° Play the mantra *"Kadosh Adonai Tzebaoth"*. You can easily find it on video platforms. Choose one that you feel comfortable listening to. Let this mantra play softly over the room until the end of the meditation at a volume that's gentle on your ears.

02.° Sitting or lying down, relax and breathe deeply for a few moments. Begin the process of relaxing your feet, legs, torso, shoulders, hands, arms, back, neck and head. Gently relaxing and releasing tension from each one. Always take deep breaths in the process, until you feel that your body and spirit are completely relaxed and calm. A feeling of calm will take over your being, keep breathing deeply until this feeling arises. It is advisable to calm your spiritual, emotional, sentimental, mental and spiritual bodies. Relaxing them all completely. Just stay in the present moment and let your body enter a deeply relaxed state. Focusing only on your breathing throughout the process.

03.° Say the following invocation out loud:

"I (state your full name), invoke the beloved presence of God the Father and Mother. I invoke the Beloved Cosmic Christ and the Planetary Christ. I invoke the Divine Holy Spirit, the Beloved

Universe and my Higher Self. That they may assist me here and now in this meditation back to the past in the beatitudes of the Beloved Christ."

04.° Now mentally say the following prayer:

"From the point of light of the mind of God. May light flow into the minds of men. And may light descend to Earth. From the point of love in the heart of God. May love flow into the hearts of men. May Christ return to Earth. From the center where God's will is known, may purpose guide the small wills of men. Purpose that the masters know and serve. From the center of what we call the race of men, may the plan of love and light be realized. And may the door to evil be closed. May light, love and power re-establish the divine plan on Earth, today and for all eternity, amen."

05.° Do the following meditation:

Slowly begin to visualize a hill by the Sea of Galilee. The land is the color of clay. It was a clear, sunny day with a blue sky overhead. There were few clouds in the sky, and small winds seemed to soften the heat in the area.

Visualize a tall man with long dark brown hair and black skin, wearing a simple suit from the time. His time-worn sandals covered his feet and protected them from the hot earth. This man appeared to be around 30 years old on average. He looked a little nervous in front of the crowd.

You are in the middle of this crowd, visualize yourself standing or sitting on the hill, where you can hear the sound of the sea in your ears. You are wearing the typical clothes of the time, very simple clothes that serve the purpose of your existence in this place. You look closely at this man, on top of this hill. He's looking out over the crowd of souls waiting for manna from heaven to fall on their heads.

You can see the people settling in, the vast majority of them standing up, others covering the floor with cloths so as not to get their worn-out clothes dirty. They speak in a language you can't understand, but that doesn't matter. Because you understand the essence of their words, deep down in their soul.

This man, Jesus Christ. He closes his eyes as a way of controlling his yearnings. And you realize that a white light begins to shine in his head. Something supernatural begins to happen. A message from heaven descends to earth at this moment, and Yeshua begins to pronounce the Beatitudes to his disciples.

"And he opened his mouth and taught them, saying:"

Blessed are the poor in spirit, for theirs is the kingdom of heaven;"

"Blessed are those who mourn, for they will be comforted;"

"Blessed are the meek, for they shall inherit the earth;"

"Blessed are those who hunger and thirst for righteousness, for they shall be filled;"

"Blessed are the merciful, for they shall obtain mercy;"

"Blessed are the clean of heart, for they shall see God;"

"Blessed are the peacemakers, for they will be called children of God;"

"Blessed are those who suffer persecution for righteousness' sake, for theirs is the kingdom of heaven;"

"Blessed are you when they revile you and persecute you, and when they lie and say all kinds of evil against you because of me."

"Rejoice and be glad, for your reward is great in heaven, for so they persecuted the prophets who were before you."

Matthew 5:2-12

Every word spoken by this man resonates so deeply in your being that you begin to see particles of light entering your soul. What comes out of Christ's mouth is poured out in abundance on the whole crowd present. You begin to realize a lightness in your spirit. Dark energies of pain, hurt, prejudice, loss, unfulfilled love, regret and even something akin to dark threads and chains begin to detach from your soul. Just let go of what needs to be cleansed from your being at this time. These energies are released, and released, and released. As Yeshua utters the Beatitudes, for long lives, you begin to feel clean. And more and more, you become more receptive to the words and the light that comes from Christ. And this light fills you and fills you with an indescribable sensation.

As Jesus continues to pronounce his beatitudes, you feel a sense of peace deepening in your heart. The people around you look at him intently, their eyes overwhelmed by the wisdom emanating from his ears. Their hearts tremble at something they haven't seen or felt before. Something supernatural is happening here; let it flow.

In the face of all the events taking place on this mountain, by the Sea of Galilee, in the face of all the waves of light where Christ is filled at this moment. You see your body filled with a deep white light. A brilliant golden flame ignites in your heart, like a flame of light that dances to the rhythm of Jesus' voice. This light expands, and expands, and expands around your body. You breathe deeply. As you look at the mountain, Christ smiles sweetly at you and speaks a word of wisdom to your being...

Slowly, you return to your body. With all the light you have gained, something like a golden sphere is over your being. You breathe deeply and thank Yeshua for his support and for the opportunity to be with him at the Sermon on the Mount.

Activating the Maharic Shield

The Maharic shield is a personal protection technique that aims to activate a protective field in the form of a pillar of silver-white light around us. It is a technique widely practiced by seekers of spiritual ascension because it is connected to an interstellar energy passed down from galactic brothers and sisters such as the Arcturians, Pleiadean's, Sirians and so on. It is an excellent exercise for activating the minor and major chakras, as well as helping planet Earth during its energetic activation due to the movement of the light of the Merkabah star in the core of our planet. To carry out this technique, we need to follow these steps:

1.° Choose music that is calm, serene and sweet to your ears during the practice. Mantras provide great spiritual support in these moments by attracting good energies and creating a harmonious field around us. Choose your mantra of choice, or if possible, listen to the famous mantra "Kadosh Adonai Tzebaoth". There are countless versions of this mantra on the internet, so choose one that is pleasing to your soul in this process.

2.° Start by relaxing your body completely:

2.1° Sit comfortably in a chair or lie down on the bed, keeping your back straight and your legs in a comfortable state for your body.

2.2° Close your eyes gently and start breathing deeply through your nose. Feel the air slowly filling your lungs and exhale through your nose or mouth. Use the color blue during your breathing, breathing in a soft, peaceful blue as it fills your lungs, and exhaling this energy slowly.

2.3° To facilitate this process, just feel yourself breathing in the blue of the sky. It brings a deep sense of calm, gentleness and freedom. Breathe in that blue and exhale calmly. Maintain this colorful breathing until the end of this exercise.

2.4° Focus your attention on your feet. Feel the tension dissipating as you relax your toes, soles and ankles. Then move to the legs, gradually relaxing the muscles, releasing any built-up tension.

2.5° Bring your attention to your torso. Allow the muscles in your abdomen and back to loosen up. Go down through your shoulders, releasing any stiffness. Let them sink gently.

2.6° Release the tension in your arms, from your shoulders to your hands. Feel each finger relaxing. Let your arms rest comfortably beside your body.

2.7° Feel your spine relaxing, vertebra by vertebra. Let your back muscles release. Move your attention to your neck, allowing it to become light and free of tension.

2.8° Release facial tension. Relax your forehead, jaw and the muscles around your eyes. Feel your head becoming lighter as the tension dissipates.

2.9° Return to deep breathing. Feel the peaceful rhythm of your breathing. Enjoy this state of relaxation for a few minutes.

3.° Say the following invocation out loud:

"I (state your full name), invoke the loving presence of God the Father and Mother. The Cosmic Christ and the Holy Spirit. I invoke the Ascended Masters of the interplanetary and cosmic hierarchy. Ashtar Command and Commander Ashtar Sheran, my sacred and powerful divine guides and mentors. The beloved Archangel Metratron and my powerful and beloved I AM Presence. So that you may assist me here and now in the activation of my personal Masharic shield."

4.° Now mentally say the following prayer:

"From the point of light of the mind of God. May light flow into the minds of men. And may light descend to Earth. From the point of love in the heart of God. May love flow into the hearts of men. May Christ return to Earth. From the center where God's will is known, may purpose guide the small wills of men. A purpose that the masters know and serve. From the center, which we call the race of men, may the plan of love and light be realized. And may the door to evil be closed. May light, love and power re-establish the divine plan on Earth today and for all eternity, amen."

5.° Visualize a six-pointed star, the flat Merkabah star made entirely of white light, positioned on your pineal gland in the exact center of your brain. Breathe gently until you can see this star.

6.° Visualizing the white Merkabah star, move it to the left side of your brain and hold it there.

7.° Now perform another visualization of a new flat Merkabah star, made entirely of silver light, positioned on your pineal gland in the exact center of your brain. Breathe gently until you can see this star.

8.° Visualizing the silver Merkabah star, move it to the right side of your brain and hold it there.

9.° Visualize now that you have two bright stars, one on each side of your brain.

10.° Move the two stars slowly towards each other and visualize the two stars merging to form a three-dimensional Merkabah star of silvery white light.

11.° Visualize the Merkabah star descending down your spine, leaving your base chakra and going to the center of the Earth. To do this, we must carry out the following steps:

11.1° Visualize this Merkabah star of silver-white light in the center of your crown chakra, located at the top of your head. Visualize this star pulsating and radiating a very strong silver-white light that shines like a sacred fire. Purifying and cleansing your head of all darkness, negativity, distorted thoughts, mental illnesses, sores, etc. When you feel you need to continue, or when you feel that the crown chakra has been properly cleansed, move on to the next stage.

11.2° Visualize this Merkabah star of silvery-white light descending from your crown chakra to your third eye chakra, located in the center of your forehead. Visualize this star pulsating and radiating a very strong silver-white light that shines like a sacred fire. Purifying and cleansing your spiritual vision of all darkness, illusions, blindness, difficulties in facing reality, etc. When you feel you need to continue, or when you feel that the chakra has been properly cleansed, move on to the next stage.

11.3° Visualize this Merkabah star of silvery-white light descending from your third eye chakra to your throat chakra, situated in the center of your neck. Visualize this star pulsating and radiating a very strong silver-white light that shines like a sacred fire. It purifies and cleanses your throat of all darkness, blockages to your expression, speech, illnesses, sores and so on. When you feel you need to continue, or when you feel that the chakra has been properly cleansed, move on to the next stage.

11.4° Visualize this Merkabah star of silver-white light descending from your throat chakra to your heart chakra, located in the center of your chest. Visualize this star pulsating and radiating a very strong silver-white light that shines like a sacred fire. Purifying and cleansing your heart of all darkness, distorted feelings, sorrows, anger, wrath, fears, desires for revenge and so on. When you feel you need to continue, or when you feel that the chakra has been properly cleansed, move on to the next stage.

11.5° Visualize this Merkabah star of silvery-white light descending from your heart chakra to your solar plexus chakra, situated a little below your chest. Visualize this star pulsating and radiating a very strong silver-white light that shines like a sacred fire. Purifying and cleansing your inner sun of all darkness, gloom, lack of will, low self-esteem, cleansing your persona and healing in the sacred flames and so on. When you feel you need to continue, or when you feel the chakra has been properly cleansed, move on to the next stage.

11.6° Visualize this Merkabah star of silvery-white light descending from your solar plexus chakra to your sacral chakra, located in your navel. Visualize this star pulsating and radiating a very strong silver-white light that shines like a sacred fire. Purifying and cleansing your energy center of all darkness, deviant desires, unbalanced emotions and so on. When you feel you need to continue, or when you feel that the chakra has been properly cleansed, move on to the next stage.

11.7° Visualize this Merkabah star of silvery-white light descending from your sacral chakra to your base chakra, situated between your genitals and your buttocks. Visualize this star pulsating and radiating a very strong silver-white light that shines like a sacred fire. Purifying and cleansing your energy center of all darkness, dark desires, unbalanced sexuality, lack of strength and courage, etc. When you feel you should continue, or when you feel the chakra has been properly cleansed, move on to the next stage.

11.8° Visualize the Merkabah star of silver-white light coming out of your base chakra, which has already been properly purified, and descending vertically over the ground until it reaches the center of the Earth. Visualize it passing through the ground and descending deeper and deeper, penetrating all the layers, earths and rocks of our globe until it finally reaches its destination.

12.° When your star reaches the center of the Earth, visualize it spinning faster and faster. Producing an enormous amount of silver-white light that covers the entire Earth in the process. Visualize the planet being taken over by a powerful radiant silver-white flame that covers the entire globe in this great sacred light. Breathe deeply until you have fully achieved this visualization.

12.1° Visualize planet Earth being cleansed and purified by the powerful silver-white flame of the star Merkabah. Its silver-white flames cover the entire globe, sweeping away all the darkness and negativity on this Earth. Hold the visualization for as long as you wish, when you feel you must continue, or when you feel the planet has been purified, proceed with the activation of the shield.

13.° Breathe deeply and draw the energies of the Merkabah star towards you. Visualize this powerful silver-white energy coming out of the Merkabah star and covering your being as you breathe in. As you exhale, move this energy back to the Merkabah star in the center of the Earth. Repeat this process three times.

14.° Now pull the energy of the Merkabah star down to thirty centimeters below your feet. Forming a silver-white circle of protection below the ground. Visualize this circle as a deep, luminous light shining down on you. It's OK to pull the energy and have it stay below a floor, ground or place where you are. If you are doing this practice lying down, visualize it below the ground, forming a circle of luminous protection that covers your entire body.

15.° Visualize the star Merkabah, which is in the center of the Earth, rising to where you are. Stopping exactly where its powerful silver-white shield is. Always visualize its great light and its faster-than-light rotation.

16.° With the star thirty centimeters below your feet. Perform the activation conjuration of your Maharic shield three times:

"I activate my Maharic shield at 100% now". 3x

17.° Visualize the Merkabah star rising and traveling throughout your body. Entering at the base chakra, going up your spine, going through all the chakras until it stops five meters above your head. As the star rises from the ground and travels through your body, visualize a powerful all or pillar of luminous light forming from the silver-white circle that grows and expands until it completely envelops you.

18.° Visualize this all of silver-white light with a circular base thirty centimeters below your feet. Five meters above your head. This is your Maharic shield.

19.° Repeat the conjuration three times:

"I activate my Maharic shield at 100% now". 3x

20.° Say the closing prayer of the activation:

"I (Say your name), give thanks for the loving presence of God the Father and Mother. The Cosmic Christ and the Holy Spirit. I thank the Ascended Masters of the interplanetary and cosmic hierarchy. I thank Command Ashtar, and Commander Ashtar Sheran. I thank my sacred and powerful divine guides and mentors. The beloved Archangel Metratron and my powerful and beloved I AM Presence. For helping me to activate my personal and planetary Maharic shield." End.

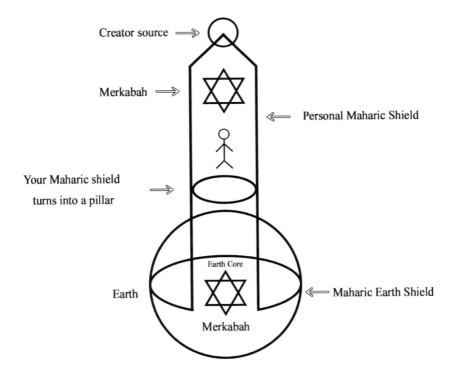

The 72 Names of God

The 72 names of God are a set of three letters derived from verses 19, 20 and 21 of the fourteenth chapter of Exodus:

"And the angel of God, who went before the host of Israel, departed, and went after them; and the pillar of cloud departed from before them, and stood behind them."

"And it went between the camp of the Egyptians and the camp of Israel; and the cloud was darkness to them, and it was light in the night to them; so that they came not near one another all the night."

"Then Moses stretched out his hand over the sea, and the Lord caused the sea to be driven back by a strong east wind all that night; and the sea became dry, and the waters were broken up."

Exodus 14:19-21.

In Hebrew, respectively:

וַיִּסַּע מַלְאַךְ הָאֱלֹהִים הַהֹלֵךְ לִפְנֵי מַחֲנֵה יִשְׂרָאֵל וַיֵּלֶךְ
מֵאַחֲרֵיהֶם וַיִּסַּע עַמּוּד הֶעָנָן מִפְּנֵיהֶם וַיַּעֲמֹד מֵאַחֲרֵיהֶם:

וַיָּבֹא בֵּין | מַחֲנֵה מִצְרַיִם וּבֵין מַחֲנֵה יִשְׂרָאֵל וַיְהִי הֶעָנָן
וְהַחֹשֶׁךְ וַיָּאֶר אֶת־הַלָּיְלָה וְלֹא־קָרַב זֶה אֶל־זֶה כָּל־הַלָּיְלָה:

וַיֵּט מֹשֶׁה אֶת־יָדוֹ עַל־הַיָּם וַיּוֹלֶךְ יְהֹוָה | אֶת־הַיָּם בְּרוּחַ
קָדִים עַזָּה כָּל־הַלַּיְלָה וַיָּשֶׂם אֶת־הַיָּם לֶחָרָבָה וַיִּבָּקְעוּ הַמָּיִם:

In the derivation of these three verses, through a process of organizing the Hebrew letters, by a process called Boustrophedon, the 72 divine names of God are obtained. These are associated with the manifestations of God along the paths of the Kabbalistic Tree of

Life. Each name represents a divine power to be manifested on our paths, each name represents a vibratory energy that, when accessed, promotes internal vibrational changes, the individual's own vibrational field is magnetized with the energies of God's divine name.

There is a faith and devotion around the world when people chant these names as a way of connecting with God. People vividly breathe these letters into their bodies, paying attention to every vibration of their speech as they chant a sacred name of the Lord letter by letter. We know that these practices are highly beneficial to the human being, as they access letters of light and power, which are strengthened daily by the faith and devotion of thousands of people around the world.

These sacred, divine or holy names are bathed in a powerful light, an energy directed towards God, a force directed towards creation. To use these names is to co-create a new reality, to be God in action, to manifest his power in our lives. For those who have their spiritual vision open, they can clearly see the celestial energies vibrating in each name, sometimes as beams of yellow and golden light. Similar to sparks or rays of sacred fire. They are living energies that, when accessed, break through the darkness of the physical world and open up a new path for the lives of their practitioners, through effort and devotion.

The 72 names of God are used in this work as a form of meditative chant. By meditating on the words, on the letters of God's name, we access its energies and bring it into our lives. By singing, we raise our vibrational frequency and elevate our current spiritual state. Indeed, they seem to promote a certain cleansing in our energy field, removing impurities from the soul and reconciling our essence with the divine Creator.

These names are separated syllable by syllable, just as you were instructed in the previous chapters of the sacred mantras and the explanations of the seals of the beatitudes and their divine names. They are in harmonious sequence and ready to be chanted.

Always starting with the mantra OM for activation, and then a real prayer to the Lord. At the end, we chant the name of Yeshua to close the cycle in salvation and radiant golden energy.

We know that the names of the Creator are a much talked about and widely debated topic on this Earth. We wanted to convey that it is a true spiritual practice for the upliftment of your souls. When I say true, I'm simply reinforcing that when we connect with God, his names and letters, we actually access a sacred energy. When the sacred begins to be part of our lives, our lives also begin to vibrate in this radiant holiness. This naturally brings about good and great changes in each person's life. The form is simple, but very powerful. For those who wish to become more and more interested in the sacred names of God, try meditating on their names for 15 minutes every day of your life. Breathing the letters and their energies into your body, in this process, is where we acquire light, where the spirit is enlightened and everything is made new. See these letters above your heads, radiating great waves of light, breathing calmly and absorbing these waves into you.

Just chanting calmly, and vibrating each word contained in this conjuration, is enough to obtain the results of the celestial connection. Begin with the word OM, after that, follow the order of the words from left to right, top to bottom, from the number one, until the number nine, left to right, until you finish all the names.

Example:

OM - Vah - Heh - Vah - Yeh - Lah - Yeh - Sah - Yah - Teh - Ah - Lah - Men - Mah - Hah - Shah - Leh - Lah - Hah and etc.

Now, without further ado, here is the mantra of the 72 names of God for chanting and practicing this book:

The 72 Names of God - יהוה

#								
1	Vah – Heh – Vah	Yeh – Lah – Yeh	Sah – Yah – Teh	Ah – Lah – Men	Mah – Hah – Shah	Leh – Lah – Hah	Ah – Kah – Ah	Kah – Heh – Teh
2	Heh – Zah – Yah	Ah – Lah – Dah	Lah – Vah – Yeh	Hah – Hah – Ah	Yeh – Zah – Lah	Meh – Bah – Hah	Hah – Rah – Yah	Heh – Kah – Men
3	Lah – Ah – Vah	Kah – Lah – Yah	Lah – Vah – Vah	Pah – Hah – Lah	Neh – Lah – Kah	Yah – Yah – Yah	Meh – Lah – Heh	Chah – Heh – Vah
4	Neh – Tah – Heh	Hah – Ah – Ah	Yah – Reh – Tah	Shah – Ah – Heh	Reh – Yah – Yah	Ah – Vah – Meh	Leh – Kah – Beh	Vah – Shah – Rah
5	Yah – Cheh – Vah	Lah – Hah – Chah	Kah – Vah – Kah	Meh – Nah – Deh	Ah – Nah – Yah	Chah – Ah – Mah	Reh – Hah – Ah	Yah – Yah – Zah
6	Hah – Hah – Hah	Mih – Yah – Kah	Vah – Vah – Lah	Yeh – Lah – Hah	Seh – Ah – Lah	Ah – Rah – Yeh	Ah – Shah – Lah	Mih – Yah – Hah
7	Vah – Heh – Vah	Deh – Nah – Yah	Hah – Chah – Shah	Ah – Meh – Meh	Neh – Nah – Ah	Neh – Yah – Tah	Mih – Bah – Hah	Peh – Vah – Yeh
8	Neh – Mah – Mah	Yeh – Yah – Lah	Hah – Rah – Chah	Mih – Tzar – Rah	Uh – Mah – Bah	Yah – Hah – Hah	Ah – Nah – Vah	Mah – Chah – Yah
9	Dah – Beh – Mah	Meh – Noh – Kah	Ah – Yah – Ah	Chah – Beh – Vah	Rah – Ah – Hah	Yah – Bah – Mah	Hah – Yah – Yah	Meh – Vah – Meh

The Golden Star

Much can be said about the Golden Star; however, it can only be felt by those who practice this personal and planetary healing technique. I believe that this technique is a new way of connecting and tuning in to what the practitioner wants to achieve or heal in their life. It has been channeled by mentors and Angels who aim to bring the Christe light of unconditional love to this Earth. As previously mentioned, the Creator aims to bring light to this world in every way, and the sacred energies of love are one of the most beautiful ways of illuminating the darkness that has resided here for long periods of time.

The Golden Star aims to illuminate the person inner self by bathing their seven bodies in a deep golden light related to ascension and divine perfection. The color gold is associated with divine wisdom, enlightenment, completeness, understanding, comprehension of all things, it is the color of the sages and one of the most sublime elevations. It is the force that great ascended masters of pure light carry in their subtle bodies. They are true receptacles of illumination, where this golden energy is seen as a brilliant radiant sun that illuminates and dispels all darkness. The golden-yellow light is one of the deepest touches of love and represents perfect spiritual illumination on the paths of light. It brings with it all knowledge, all wisdom and understanding about life, the universes and the divine Creator. Those who possess these radiations naturally know God in action deeply.

Buddha is seen and represented in yellow and gold tones, as are all his disciples and servants who follow the same path to enlightenment. For in himself, Siddhartha Gautama is a soul with very high evolution and spiritual knowledge. The color gold vibrates in completeness enlightenment, when the initiate reaches the highest degree of his spiritual evolution. They become complete in life and no longer have any need to experience trials in an earthly world.

These bearers of the golden light (and also the violet light) are great Masters who coordinate planets, galaxies and constellations. They are fully ascended consciousnesses and vibrate on a much larger scale than we know in this world. In order to have the wisdom and honor of coordinating a planetary sphere, one must have evolved greatly and caused a great change in it. That's why Christ is considered the planetary ruler of this world. Already an Ascended spirit before incarnating, he completed himself in light by going through the trials of this world and became completely golden by encompassing all the colors, all the rays of the Creator, all divine perfection and essence. It became completely golden in its essence.

The Golden Star emerges as a facilitating process for practitioners to ascend spiritually by illuminating their bodies and situations that vibrate in a non-harmonious state in their lives. They become true bearers of the golden healing light by manifesting this golden light in their lives and throughout the world. By channeling the golden energy into their bodies, thus making a quantum leap and awaken to new realities the likes of which they have never experienced in their lives.

As you awaken, the light increases in your bodies, and as you light up, you will realize that a new life is present in your daily life. You will vibrate at a new frequency and will be able to see the Earth, nature and the touch of the Creator as never before. Simply because you are now in tune with a higher energy that can bring great miracles into your lives. The Golden Star comes to this world as a way of sharing the light of the Creator and the light of Christ on Earth, at times when it has never been so necessary for this light to grow up and expand through the afflicted hearts of those who seek some loving touch in their souls.

The more we bathe this world in this Star, the more the world will be able to heal itself and speed up the process of planetary transition that has been taking place for a long time. As a healing technique, it allows us to heal through enlightenment all the disharmonies that may be present on our paths. Not limited to time and space, it can heal such ancient aspects of our essence, and at the same time heal events from the past that still reverberate in our minds. Only one change is needed for a pattern to be broken and a soul to be freed from such ancient weights that they have been carrying on their backs for millennia.

This technique is not only based on golden energy as its Master, but we also tune in to our Sun Star, which warms and illuminates this world. In all beliefs, the sun has always been seen as a masculine figure of such beauty and completeness. Surrounded by the most beautiful things, the most beautiful gadgets, the highest values, the highest hierarchies. Associated with the thrones of kings, the prosperity of empires, the unparalleled beauty of the brilliance and splendor of the heavens. The sun is the representative of life, the one who warms the soul, brings breath to the soul, makes us breathe to live. It is life itself, so powerful and incomparable.

It is in joy that we can live, in light that we can be happy, in splendor that we can illuminate ourselves. Like the sun that warms all cold, by bringing this energy into our bodies, we are bringing the energy and light of life into our lives. By tuning in to this energy, we are bringing its purifying fire to our essence, bringing its light to illuminate our paths. We are bringing the fire that warms all the coldness and illuminates all the darkness of our essence.

When a soul is in a negative state, wounded physically, mentally, emotionally or spiritually, either by life's sorrows, by their own actions or by insisting on dark paths, their spiritual bodies become dark. The lack of light manifests itself in shades of black, gray and sometimes an opaque dark blue becomes present in their aura. We can also see opaque red tones in aggressive auras or those who have committed murder, mutilation and barbarity by breaking with the subtleties of the soul for bloodthirsty and destructive ways. Normally, black and gray are the most predominant colors, and the vibration of black in particular is unanimous in spirits that are negative and considered evil. However, this color can also appear in cases of depression, fear, anxiety, destructive desires and perversities of the soul. I see that it seems to be an infinite cycle, where this color only manifests in these hearts, and when souls are under the regency of this vibration, they only become something they are not.

Therefore, by bringing the sun's energies into these bodies, if you are vibrating at this low frequency, you can purify your essence from these energy densities and free your soul from feeling unconnected to creation. The golden vibrations and fire of the sun will naturally heal these inner wounds and illuminate your densified bodies so that you can breathe a sigh of relief. Likewise, when a great sense of heaviness is lifted from your bodies, you will finally be able to breathe in peace.

The sun, the representative of joy, peace, enlightenment, life, prosperity, physical and spiritual riches, beatitudes, enlightened paths, endless happiness and love, the light that warms the soul, the love that sings in the chest, the manifestation of all the good things in this world and all the upliftment and salvation of this Earth. By bringing these energies into your bodies on a daily basis, can you understand how great your journey would be if you were bathed in sun light? By receiving the touch of life, you too can live. By feeling the warm breath of life, you will know that life is beautiful and full of the pleasures and joys that the soul so longs to experience.

So far, I think you have understood the greatness of the power of the golden-yellow ray. But there is a color tone, a ray from the creator, which is greater and more evolved than the golden color. It is known as the violet flame, and this, dear friends, is the provider of the greatest wonders in our lives. The famous and powerful violet flame of Saint Germain, Master of the seventh ray of the creator, is an extremely strong tool for cleansing karmas, healing, purification and ascension of the soul through its powerful and infinite radiant color.

The violet flame is the key to planetary healing, because its vibration is extremely high, vibrating at higher powers than any other color or ray. By itself, it is able to stop the most negative processes of the soul, being a transmuter, since everything it touches transmutes and leads to the light. It breaks down negative roots, is able to heal ailments of the body and soul, transmutes situations and experiences, can stop the worst wars and cease the deepest darkness in its unparalleled flames. Its bearers are naturally beautiful, radiating its frequencies which, in spiritual vision, are similar to a great violet sun in incandescent flames.

I like to say that nothing exists but the violet flame; it is the complete union of the threefold flame of blue, yellow and pink rays. Willpower, wisdom and love, respectively. When the three flames become one, the violet flame is born, which encompasses these qualities in one and awakens its beings to a new life in spiritual enlightenment. Daily meditations with this flame seem to change our reality in a way that can only be experienced, as words are often lacking in our vocabulary to exemplify the power of this flame. It is astonishing and, at the same time, we feel complete when we emanate these flames in our spirit.

Sharing a personal experience with this flame, I was once visualizing myself surrounded by this sacred violet flame, and I felt, after a while of keeping this visualization active, something being purified in my chest. At the same moment, I received a message from a guide that a chronic illness I'd had since childhood had been cured from my lungs. Through perseverance, daily meditation and raising our consciousness, we can obtain miracles and the manifestation of healing in our lives. We don't make promises of healing, but we certainly get the support of spirituality in everything that is necessary for us to live fully in peace, happiness and health. If we are willing and allow ourselves to be uplifted, then event after event will appear in our daily lives so that everything is always taken care of by the wise hands of the spirits of light.

I see when spirits are touched by this flame. Their bodies glow a purple light. Their minds are purified and magically transformed. They seem to become other souls, completely different from their previous versions. When the violet flame hits an individual's soul, that soul will certainly be transmuted into that fire, and their entire personality will be purified to a new, higher level of consciousness. I've seen it happen more than once: when the violet fire touches, nothing can stop it.

Among the many qualities that the sacred violet flame possesses, the liberation of the soul is perhaps one of the most beautiful. It stops their pain and opens the way to a new dawn, where they can experience what God has truly prepared for them. In an unparalleled wonder, witnessing Saint Germain and his aura, which resembles a brilliant, resplendent and unparalleled sun of violet flames, is one of the greatest beauties we can see. Witnessing the auras of the ascended masters is one of the greatest wonders in the world. And to think that, with due effort and dedication, we can reach these levels and go on endlessly evolving to levels unknown to us, is something that motivates us to be better every day.

That said, the Sacred Golden Star has two complementary techniques that form it. The first is the activation of a triangle of violet fire capable of transmuting our essence and our entire body with a powerful purifying and ascending flame. The violet flame itself is capable of stopping the densest and most negative processes of the soul, being a powerful flame that encompasses all the most perfect qualities of the Creator in one shade of color. By exercising this flame in our lives, we acquire all the qualities of the Creator's rays, because all of them in their highest scales become violet as well as your divine essence.

In short, the violet flame is one of the most perfect manifestations of the creator encompassed in a powerful flame capable of cleansing, transmuting and elevating the soul to levels of consciousness never before experienced by them. This triangle activation exercise also gives us spiritual protection with a touch of divine magic as we bring the name of Jesus to our chest and protect our heart from all negative influences of the body and soul, both internal and external.

The second part of the Golden Star exercise is done by bathing our bodies in golden light. From the top of our head to our heart chakra. By bathing our essence in the golden light of Christ, we tune in to our Higher Self, allowing us to access and receive new information, soul technologies and instructions from our Higher Self. And just as my beloved Archangel Gabriel says perfectly and clearly right now:

"The color gold is the color of the Higher Self; it is the color that represents everything. Since God is everything, gold becomes perfect in his eyes, and connects us with one of the highest frequencies that exists." - Archangel Gabriel.

By bathing our essence in the powerful Golden light of Christ, we can more easily access the Divine Self and integrate our soul with our higher essence through a process of golden soul energy fusion. Attuned to a higher scale frequency, naturally our life, our paths, our essence become more alive, clean, pleasant, peaceful, prosperous, open and loving. Qualities so present in perfect worlds and in those who constantly seek their spiritual upliftment.

In this second stage of what makes up the Golden Star technique, we can expand this golden light to our requests, and this is where the magic happens. Every imbalance in our world is due to the lack of light in it. All the pain, the loss, the anger, the wars, the perdition, all the addictions, all the tears, all the suffering, all the darkness, the gloom and the abyss are just forms that don't have their own light. Just as all the problems in our lives are due to the lack of light in us. When we manage to illuminate the darkness, the darkness automatically stops its negative process and begins to harmonize and bring more good things on our paths. For example:

Let's say you're having problems with your prosperity. We can then say that the area of your finances is in disharmony. And all disharmony has dark tones, grays and dull, lifeless blues. This is the manifestation of the color vibrations that are in everything and everyone around us. By sending light to your financial area, preferably the vibration manifested in prosperity colors such as gold and yellow, it stops vibrating in dark tones and starts vibrating in tones of frequencies related to money. Consequently, your financial life starts to flow more easily and money starts to come into your life.

Another example I can give is this: let's say you're in a melancholy state, with depression, anxiety and sadness in your life.

Automatically, the spiritual vibration that is with you manifests itself through the colors black, gray, a dull and lifeless dark blue, and sometimes dull red tones are also present when anger, rage and hatred take over our being.

When we undergo an energy treatment, where we receive an energy cleansing, a discharge of dark energies or some light in our bodies, that black, dense and negative energy is removed from our spirit and a more subtle one begins to vibrate. Sometimes in white colors with brighter, happier and more radiant colored lights. This makes us more willing to live, with more disposition, joy, desires, dreams, and we begin to see life in more colors.

Prayers in a house of faith and charity, a Catholic mass, a Christian meeting, a spiritual cleansing with healers, a lit candle to our guardian angel are all ways of removing the vibrational darkness from our soul. And bathe it in lighter, peaceful, lively and serene tones. In this way, we treat these imbalances by clearing away the darkness and starting to vibrate in higher vibrational tones.

We can cite a beautiful example when a person is blocked in their love life. Usually, old people in their lives prevent them from pursuing new relationships because of energetic cords tied to them. You can also find spells, incantations, charms and even entities acting to block these paths. Speaking of colors, these cords can look like small darkened lines, thick cords of reddish colors that extend to the hearts or spiritual strongholds of negative entities. We can also see black, gray, red and dull blue colors.

When we send the energies through the Gold Star, everything that was hindering the relationship will receive a high-frequency force, healing and illuminating that area in the process. Speaking of the Gold Star, we will certainly have a healing and purifying process if used wisely. It can even, depending on the frequency and will of the practitioner, completely rid them of their turbulent past in order to experience new harmonies in their life.

Through your personal healing process, your vibration rises and understanding becomes present. When the individual begins to vibrate more intensely in love, we obtain a release from the destructive connection of past ties. Even when these ties and cords may be non-existent when we refer to people from the past, the healing of the loving and sentimental area is still fully present. For when we illuminate it, we receive light. And these light spreads, bringing new encounters, new personal understandings, new opportunities for growth and, as previously mentioned, new harmonies and experiences to be lived.

This is how an energetic vibrational change in our lives is defined, and it can be applied to every example we can think of. This is how mentors of light and sacred forces change our paths, promote happiness, joy, peace, hope, prosperity, love, open paths and good events. All through the work, the change of vibration and the illumination of our paths. As a result, through this internal healing work, our vibratory field is harmonized and we start to live with more happiness and joy in life.

Now, think how powerful it is for the person practicing this work to expand this sacred golden energy of Christ by showering planet Earth with it. By expanding and illuminating the four corners of the world with this ascensionary energy that represents the Higher Self of all of us, we are bringing this elevated consciousness into this world. And, above all, we are connecting planet Earth and its consciousness to its most divine and elevated form. The planet is a living being, it has a soul and consciousness, it is a living spiritual form just like you and me. By bathing this soul in the golden energy, you will be healing the Earth and helping it to connect with her highest Self.

Unfortunately, with humanity's destructive processes of killing nature and waging senseless wars, driven by anger and discord, wounds open up in the Earth's soul. Her vibratory field is damaged and disharmonies begin to occur on this physical realm. The result is natural catastrophes, with the influence of the stars and constellations with all planetary alignments, eclipses, full moons, stellar events, etc, these events collapse the harmful energies that have been hidden under wraps. Including those things that people avoid facing in their lives and try to pretend they don't exist. In other words, everything that hasn't been worked on by us, and by humanity as a whole. Everything that has been ignored and left out of our lives. In fact, one day they will come back in full force at the request of the universe. As a way of evolving and also as a way of learning not to run away from our consciences. When we run away from situations, we walk on dark paths of the soul. If we do it once, we'll do it again and again. An energetic snowball effect is created, and it becomes increasingly difficult to regain the strength, determination, power and maturity to face our suffering and resolve it once and for all.

It's the same with nations, where fights are silent until they explode and lives are lost in the process. May man be able to resolve his situations without hurting anyone. May mankind be able to feel God's love in their hearts, free from the bonds that imprison them in the dark boxes of creation. May humanity feel the peace of God's kingdom. And to know that everything has a solution in their lives. If everyone felt love, love would take them in its hands and guide them to the most beautiful and blissful places of the soul. Where there is no sadness, pain, suffering, sorrow or scarcity. Only love is lived and experienced in our lives. Such is the life of all the Masters who have ascended by going through this incarnational experience that you find yourselves in. But fear not, why fear? Why be afraid of life? Why fear love and happiness? Why run, my beloved? Just live, and watch the sun rise through your windows every day. And for those who have the opportunity, look out over a beautiful, peaceful beach at the touch of dawn. If you only knew how wonderful God's works are. How perfect the Creator's graces are. How perfect it is to be with God and feel him in our bodies. They would then know that the greatest desire of their lives is to be able to live. And to be alive to experience it. I am Saint Germain, and I bid you farewell. Thank you, my beloved souls of the Creator. You are very much loved, don't forget that. I love you very much, and I thank you for all the good work done here on this plane. Halu - Saint Germain

Soon I'll give you a step-by-step guide to activating the Golden Star. Just follow the recommendations and always let the experience flow. There's no need to force yourself to visualize any of your topics. Let the whole experience flow as it should. Naturally, the exercise will run its course and perform this loving inner healing technique in your being. Some people may find it difficult to manifest images, colors or geometric shapes. Know that all this work is supported by spirituality, which will certainly help you throughout the process.

At some points on the Golden Star, you will be asked to visualize yellow or violet flames. In these cases, just visualize these flames as if they were a living fire vibrating and burning in the chosen color. There is no need to fear aspects of the flesh, as the fire will not burn in a physical way. But the element of fire on the spiritual realm possesses purifying power and will energize the practitioner in their elemental power. Promoting life, strength, vigor, drive, disposition, etc.

The vibrational color given to fire indicates the energy it will manifest in your life. If it is golden, it will bring knowledge, wisdom, understanding, life, joy, strength, Christic energy, connection with the Higher Self, prosperity, abundance and so on. If its color is purple-violet, it will bring transmutation, purification, evolution, ascension, burning of karmas, liberation, quantum leap, etc. Fire in itself is a purifying tool. When associated with a particular color, it receives the energy and frequency according to the vibration of the chosen one. So, just visualize it covering your being and you being taken over by a powerful radiant fiery energy that will work to your advantage.

With your mind focused, simply visualize powerful golden or violet flames, depending on the stage of the Golden Star exercise. To make it easier, see that your chakras are like luminous spheres, see these spheres being taken up, purified and transmuted by the sacred golden and violet flames. Similar to a living ascensionary and purifying fire. This alone gives us the performance we need to bathe our chakras in these sacred high-vibration energies. Keep the visualization of the living flames purifying throughout the entire process. Over time, they will intensify as you practice them and their powers will be increasingly enhanced and made alive in our being.

Remember to practice daily to get the best results. And always leave a candle burning for the desired beatitude. The respective colors are given in each of the chapters. More information will be given in the chapter where I teach you how to activate consecrated candles for the beatitudes in a simple way.

The Golden Star method can be expanded so that you can intercede on behalf of other people with this technique. In this magical practice, we will send the sacred energies of the star's central divine name to bless and bring light. There are many ways to use the Golden Star, both for personal use and for energetic healing of people, situations, places, timelines, planets, etc. Some examples that can be given are:

- You can send the energies to the past, helping to heal and release old things.

- You can send the energies to animals, vegetation, forests, springs or anywhere in the natural world.

- You can send the energies to the deva worlds of the elementals, to increase your connections with the elements and bless the divine spirits.

- You can send the energies to ancestors, spirit guides and any entity you wish to help, heal or bless.

- You can send the energies to solve any problem. Just in the act of healing, all darkness becomes light.

- You can send the energies anywhere in the world. Including the spirit world and even the Umbral (hell). To help heal the spirits that reside there.

- You can send the energies to heal parallel lines and realities. Including dimensions, levels of consciousness, triggers that activate destructive timelines or anything that is aligned or intertwined with a negative destiny for humanity. Use the Seal of Yeshua provided at the end of the book for this.

- You can send the energies for planetary healing. Covering the whole Earth with the golden light of Christ.

- And of course, you can send it to people, family members, acquaintances, friends, strangers in the street and so on.

The Golden Star – Practice

01.° Activate your Maharic Shield.

02.° Perform the conjuration of the 72 Names of God.

03.° Say the opening prayer:

"I (Say your name), ask for the intercession of the Divine Cosmic Christ, the Divine Planetary Christ, my Higher Self, the Holy Spirit and the Beloved Universe. May you help me in this meditation, and may your light govern this divine work".

04.° Think about what you want to achieve. What do you want to change, heal, manifest, cleanse, regenerate, etc. Both internal and external changes are valid at this time.

05.° Meditate on the divine seal of the desired beatitude. Containing the divine name that will be worked on in this process. Run your eyes over the Hebrew letters contained there. Connect with the divine forces that govern this sacred meditation.

06.° Mentalize the divine seal above your head. It shines a radiant golden light that covers your entire body and the place where you are standing. The golden light represents the Christ consciousness of purity and unconditional love.

- It is not necessary to visualize all the names in Hebrew. Therefore, take the time to connect with the divine seal and all the sacred names contained therein.

- Concentrate on the central name of the divine seal.

- Visualize the divine seal shining in golden light.

07.° Visualize that, through the divine seal, a great pyramid of violet fire is forming high up in the sky. It is large enough to cover your entire body and the place where you are. The pyramid is made up entirely of violet flames, inside and out. Bring this pyramid of violet fire vertically, from the top of the heavens to you, until this sacred pyramid has perfectly enveloped all your bodies and your essence in a tremendous violet flame.

08.° The pyramid has transmutative and purifying properties. Visualize the three Maltese crosses in pure violet fire. Over the energy center of your heart. Forming a flat triangle of burning sacred flames. The triangle takes shape until it is complete. Forming a perfect flat pyramid in your heart with the sacred names on it.

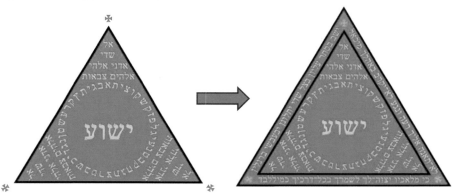

The main focus of this triangle are the Maltese crosses, the sacred symbolism of the beloved Master Saint Germain, which embody the qualities of the violet flame. And the powerful name of Yeshua, the Christ, within the sacred triangle. We must visualize the crosses, the golden circle of the 42 divine names and, in its center, the name of the beloved Master Jesus on our chest. Shining and glowing with the powerful golden flame of Ascension and the fullness of life. In this way, you will correctly incorporate this technique and transmute your divine essence into the powerful violet-golden flame of Christ.

As for the other names and verses in gold, they are complementary to this technique. If you can visualize all of them perfectly, it will be of great value. To do this, take the time to connect with the symbology of the triangle and, when practicing, simply bring it to your chest directly from this book you're reading. Or if you prefer, create one with the power of your mind and just connect with the symbolism you've meditated on.

It is also very useful to *"breathe in"* the image of this seal and visualize it entering your heart. There, where it should pulsate its light and protect your energy center. Through this technique, we protect our heart, our most valuable asset, against the forces of darkness, we heal it through the energy of Christ and we ensure that our feelings are always purified so that we can be the infinite light that we have come to be in this world.

Too often, our lives are diverted from their focus by false loves, false promises, desires and wounds from the past, where our heart, the energy center that naturally distributes energies to all the other chakras, becomes dirty; with dark spirits and entities lodged in it, and increasingly cold. This is a natural consequence of all those who run away from their feelings and their conscience, where they close their eyes to the light and create ways out of facing their learning and challenges.

Protecting the heart is protecting the soul. It's protecting your divine essence so that the pain and darkness of the world doesn't enter your spirit and you aren't controlled by the enemies of the sanctified soul.

8.1° Visualize yourself inside the great pyramid, keeping the triangle of violet crosses over your heart active in your memory. Visualize yourself being purified by the sacred violet flame. Just perceiving, or simply connecting. Visualize all your 7 chakras and your 7 spiritual bodies being bathed, transmuted and purified by this sacred violet flame.

8.2° Remain in this visualization, where your entire body, your life, the air you breathe, all your organs, your blood, your cells, your bones, the entire length of your bodies, all your karma, all your debts of conscience, all evil, all guilt, all mistakes, all anger, all grief, all unhappiness, everything that is out of harmony in your life and your entire soul become living violet flames that purify and transmute everything and everyone they touch. In time, you will incorporate the qualities of the violet flame into your essence, and through this technique you will be able to transmute your whole life into a perfect sacred flame. The longer you stay with this technique, the better the results will be.

You can even reactivate the sacred pyramid in the center of your chest after completing this technique as a form of energetic and spiritual protection against emergency situations or whenever you need spiritual support. To do this, simply place your hands in the center of your chest, forming a sacred triangle of violet flames. And in its center, visualize Yeshua's name glowing in golden flames. Take a deep breath and activate the following spiritual command:

"Expand Pyramid of Christic Protection." 3x

"Yeshua Hamashiah." 3x

"Visualize this pyramid expanding until it covers your entire body. Visualize yourself inside a triangle completely formed by burning violet flames. And in its center, shines the powerful golden flame of the Christ."

09.° While visualizing the divine seal on the top of your head. Bring it with the force of your thought to the center of your chest, where your heart chakra is located.

9.1° Calmly visualize this golden seal radiating its light over your head. It slowly descends, entering and passing through your crown chakra. It turns into a brilliant golden fire. Visualize this seal as a powerful golden flame, which touches and purifies your energy center with a powerful radiant flame. Maintain this golden fire visualization until your chakra has been bathed in this powerful golden flame of Christ.

"For all those who feel it in their hearts. Instead of using the name of beatitude in the angelic seals. You can use the Hebrew name of Christ - Yeshua in the visualization of the golden sphere entering your bodies and illuminating them completely. This seal is available at the end of this book. It can be used as a Master Seal to activate all the beatitudes described here."

9.2° After visualizing and feeling that your crown chakra has been transformed into a powerful flaming golden sphere. Move the seal to the third eye chakra, located in the center of your forehead, transforming it into a brilliant golden fire. Visualize this seal as a powerful golden flame that touches and purifies your energy center with a powerful radiant flame. Maintain this golden fire visualization until your chakra has been bathed in this powerful golden flame of Christ.

The flames dance at a fast pace and a golden circle form in the center of your forehead. It radiates powerful waves of golden light all around. The shape of the golden circle should be as follows:

Symbol of the Sun.

It should be visualized in the shape of a circle of golden flames over the third eye chakra.

9.3° Once you have formed the circle of golden fire on your forehead. Lower the sacred seal to your throat chakra. Located in the center of the larynx, it turns into a brilliant golden fire. Visualize this seal as a powerful golden flame that touches and purifies your energy center with a powerful radiant flame. Maintain this golden fire visualization until your chakra has been bathed in this powerful golden flame of Christ.

9.4° When you feel that your whole voice and chakra have been transformed into a powerful sphere of golden flame. Lower the sacred seal to the center of your chest. Where the heart chakra is, transform it into a brilliant golden fire. Visualize this seal as a powerful golden flame that touches and purifies your energy center with a powerful radiant flame. The flames dance at a fast pace, forming the powerful eight-petaled flower of the Anahata chakra in the form of a golden fire over your body. Visualize this fiery golden lotus flower opening up and enveloping you. Then focus your attention on the golden flames of Christ and visualize them taking over your whole body. Feel your soul being touched and bathed by these powerful radiant flames, visualizing the whole of your being being bathed, transmuted and blessed by the powerful golden flames of Christ. Stay in this visualization for a few moments until you feel that this golden fire has been properly encompassed in your being. Until you feel that your soul shines with an unparalleled golden radiance, similar to the sweet glow of the sun.

10.° Read the Bible verse and start chanting the sacred mantra of the beatitude verse as harmoniously as possible. Repeat chanting the mantra until you feel its effects manifesting in your body and life. Remember to sing harmoniously. As if you were singing to God, in full joy and youth to the Heavenly Father.

11.° Concentrate on your desire and visualize it being taken over by this sacred golden flame and totally bathed, healed and manifested by this divine light.

12.° Remain in this golden meditative state for a few moments. Naturally, the golden energies will become more and more incorporated into your essence as you practice. Keep your attention solely on your breathing, inhaling and exhaling this golden energy that is flowing throughout your body at this moment, in your veins, in your organs, in all your chakras, in your mind, in your spirit, in your body and in your request.

13.° Expand the golden radiation to the whole Earth. Visualize the planet being filled with this radiant light. Visualize planet Earth being completely covered by a powerful golden flame. This golden flame covers the entire globe, vibrating a radiant, luminous and powerful golden flame. To facilitate this meditation. At this stage, follow these steps:

13.1° Sitting down, in a comfortable position. Place your two hands with the palms facing upwards.

13.2° Visualize holding planet Earth gently with your hands. Resting it on your lap. Likewise, when you hold a sphere at its base.

13.3° When you expand the golden light to the whole Earth. Simply visualize the planet being taken over by a radiant golden light. This light is like a golden fire that shines, purifies and illuminates this world.

13.4° Just let the flames flow naturally. There is no need to force or "push" the flames into the earth. This happens naturally and peacefully.

13.5° In due course. You will observe your own soul taken by a luminous glow. And the Earth in your hands, seized by a radiant golden flame.

13.6° When you feel you need to end the meditation. Just do it. Hold out your hands and place the Earth in front of you. As if you were handing it over to the universe. Then join your two hands and say the following prayer:

14.° Closing prayer:

"I (say your name), thank the Divine Cosmic Christ, the Divine Planetary Christ, my Higher Self, the Holy Spirit and the Beloved Universe. For the opportunity to manifest the light in my life. And for the expansion of your light on this Earth, amen.".

Return to your day as normal and try to keep your thoughts elevated.

Sending the Golden Energy

At this stage, you will be instructed on how to send these sacred energies to others. Remember that this technique has no space-time limitations, and you can act freely to help whomever you wish. The possibilities of this golden technique are endless. Anyone who receives this force, whether animate or not, will receive the attunement of the golden star. And they will receive the Christic energies of the beatitudes in their bodies. To do this, follow these steps:

01.° Activate your Maharic Shield.

02.° Perform the conjuration of the 72 Names of God.

03.° Say the opening prayer:

"I (Say your name), ask for the intercession of the Divine Cosmic Christ, the Divine Planetary Christ, from my Higher Self, the Holy Spirit and the Beloved Universe. May you help me in this meditation, and may your light govern this divine work".

04.° Think about what you want to achieve. What do you want to change, heal, manifest, cleanse, regenerate, etc. Both internal and external changes are valid at this time.

05.° Meditate on the divine seal of the desired beatitude. Containing the divine name that will be worked on in this process. Run your eyes over the Hebrew letters contained there. Connect with the divine forces that govern this sacred meditation.

06.° Mentalize the divine seal above your head. It shines a radiant golden light that covers your entire body and the place where you are standing. The golden light represents the Christ consciousness of purity and unconditional love.

- It is not necessary to visualize all the names in Hebrew. Therefore, take the time to connect with the divine seal and all the sacred names it contains.

- Concentrate on the central name of the divine seal.

- Visualize the divine seal shining in golden light.

07.° Visualize that, through the divine seal, a great pyramid of violet fire is forming high up in the heavens. It is big enough to cover your entire body and the place where you are. The pyramid is made up entirely of violet flames, inside and out. Bring this pyramid of violet fire vertically, from the top of the heavens to you, until this sacred pyramid has perfectly encompassed all your bodies and your essence in a tremendous violet flame.

08.° The pyramid has transmutative and purifying properties. Visualize the three Maltese crosses in pure violet fire. Over the energy center of your heart. Forming a flat triangle of burning sacred flames. The triangle takes shape until it is complete. Forming a perfect flat pyramid in your heart with the sacred names on it.

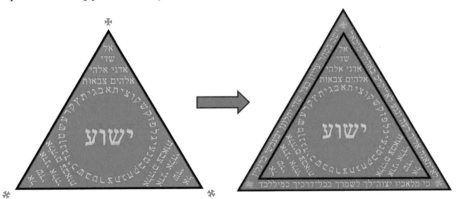

8.1° Visualize yourself inside the great pyramid, keeping the triangle of violet crosses over your heart active in your memory. Visualize yourself being purified by the sacred violet flame. Just perceiving, or simply connecting. Visualize all your 7 chakras and your 7 spiritual bodies being bathed, transmuted and purified by this sacred violet flame.

8.2° Remain in this visualization, where your entire body, your life, the air you breathe, all your organs, your blood, your cells, the entire length of your bodies, all your karma, all your debts of conscience, all evil, all guilt, all mistakes, all anger, all grief, all unhappiness, everything that is out of harmony in your life and your entire soul become living violet flames that purify and transmute everything and everyone they touch. In time, you will incorporate the qualities of the violet flame into your essence, and through this technique you will be able to transmute your whole life into a perfect sacred flame. The longer you stay with this technique, the better the results will be.

09.° With the palms of your hands facing upwards. Visualize the seal of beatitude coming down from the high heavens into the palms of your hands. It radiates a powerful golden flame. Visualize this seal as a great sphere of solar golden fire energy. Like a small big sun in the palm of your hands. This ball of light radiates a radiant golden light that covers your entire body and the place where you are.

10.° Read the Bible verse and start chanting the sacred mantra as harmoniously as possible. Repeat chanting the mantra until you feel its effects on the Golden Star. At this point, as the whole universe is moved by intention, carry out the next step:

11.° Say the following prayer of surrender of light:

"I (say your name), at this moment, ask that the divine forces of light. From the Beloved Cosmic Christ, the Beloved Planetary Christ, from my Higher Self, from the Holy Spirit and the Beloved Universe, to bring this Golden Star and its blessings to (Say the name of the person, place, situation desired, etc.). So that everything can be healed, harmonized and bathed in this divine light."

11.1° Visualize the star traveling and arriving at the indicated location. This journey is usually instantaneous. It takes less than a few milliseconds for this golden sphere to arrive at your location.

When the Golden Star reaches the person, place or situation you wish to work with. Visualize the Golden Star encompassing the person or situation you want to work on.

12.° Visualize this Golden Star completely bathing with its golden flame in a radiant Christic energy of unconditional love, elevation, purity and celestial harmony the objective worked on in this ritual. Visualize the objective being taken up by these golden solar flames and being transmuted into celestial fire within this Sacred Star. Until the whole situation/objective is duly purified and becomes golden and radiant like sunlight. Just visualize this sacred fire purifying and healing everything and everyone you want.

13.° Expand the golden radiance to the whole Earth. Visualize the planet being filled with this radiant light. Visualize planet Earth being completely covered by a powerful golden flame. This golden flame covers the entire globe, pulsating a radiant, luminous and powerful golden flame. To facilitate this meditation. At this stage, follow these steps:

13.1° Sitting down, in a comfortable position. Place your two hands with the palms facing upwards.

13.2° Visualize holding planet Earth gently with your hands. Resting it on your lap. Likewise, when you hold a sphere at its base.

13.3° When you expand the golden light to the whole Earth. Simply visualize the planet being taken over by a radiant golden light. This light is like a golden fire that shines, purifies and illuminates this world.

13.4° Just let the visualization of the flames flow naturally. There is no need to force or *"push"* the flames into the Earth. It happens naturally and peacefully.

13.5° In due time, you will see your own soul taken over by a radiant glow. And the earth in your hands, seized by an incandescent golden flame.

13.6° When you feel you need to end the meditation. Just do it. Hold out your hands and place the Earth in front of you. As if you were handing it over to the universe. Then join your two hands and say the following prayer:

14.° Closing prayer:

"I (say your name), thank the Divine Cosmic Christ, the Divine Planetary Christ, my Higher Self, the Holy Spirit and the Beloved Universe. For the opportunity to manifest the light in this work. And for the expansion of your light on this Earth, amen".

Return normally to your day and try to keep your thoughts elevated.

Activating the Beatitudes

A simple way to activate the beatitudes in our daily lives is by lighting candles to them. By blessing them to the divine Christ and all your guides and mentors, you can obtain a spiritual anchor of light on your path. By making a habit of burning a seven-day candle (Big candles, also known as pillar candles, that last for seven days or more) to all our guides and mentors, I realize that this is an excellent way to maintain an active spiritual connection with our forces of light.

We all have our guides and mentors, spirits of light who accompany us on our journey and lead us on paths of evolution, learning and growth. As well as being highly beneficial for our soul, being in tune and connected with them, the act of keeping a candle lit for the light will always bring blessings in our way. Think of how a burning flame can illuminate the deepest darkness. In this symbolism, our lit candle illuminates our soul and keeps all darkness and adversity away from us, because we will always have a light to guide us in times of trouble.

The process of consecrating the candle is quite simple, as is activating the desired beatitude to enter its frequency more easily. All you need is a candle of the color indicated for each desired beatitude, or preferably a golden seven-day candle, as it is associated with the enlightenment and wisdom of the Beloved Christ.

Common white candles and golden seven-day candles are the standard candles and can be used freely for all the beatitudes in this book.

To carry out this activation, follow these simple steps:

1.° Have the beatitude you want printed, preferably in gold color. The seal can be 11x11 or 12x12 cm. It is also possible to print the beatitudes in the full size of A4 sheets, in which case I recommend that you print them out and put them on the walls of your homes. Especially in your places of prayer so that they radiate their golden and merciful energies to the place. Remember to clean them constantly with a dry cloth so that they don't accumulate dust, and if the seals get too old over time, just burn them and print new ones.

If you want a material that will last longer, the seals can be made from Ps boards, mdf wood or even printed fabric. The dimensions can vary from taste to taste, I particularly have radiesthesia charts in the size of 23x23cm and I like them a lot. There are larger sizes such as 32x32cm or more, it's up to taste. Remember that just the A4 paper with the complete seal already makes a big difference to the location, so adapt according to your needs. All the full-color Beatitudes seals will be available to download in high resolution via a link at the end of this book. Or just contact me by email at the end and I'll provide you with the link.

1.1° If you are going to use A4 paper with the seal of the desired beatitude, remember to cut out the seal and leave it without any burrs or leftover paper, leaving only the sacred seal in a circular shape. You can use crepe tape behind the seal to stick it to the wall without any problem.

2.° A candle in the color of the blessing or preferably a seven-day candle in gold color. All these candles can easily be found in religious shops.

3.° (Optional) Extra virgin olive oil, myrrh oil, nard, balsam or olibanum are great options for anointing candles and enhancing their effects. Anointing oils are easy to find online or in religious shops.

Step-by-step activation:

1.° To activate the beatitudes with the candles, simply take the candle you want and place it on an candle holder so that there are no accidents on the spot. If you're using the seven-day candle, use a candle cup specifically for this purpose, or you can improvise with metal or aluminum cups/forms easily found in convenience stores.

2.° Afterwards, place the seal of the beatitude under the candle holder so that when the candle reaches its end, you don't burn it. If candle wax gets on it, or it is damaged in any way, just burn it and make a new one. You can also place the seal on the side of the candle and add a photo of the person who will receive the energy. You can also place a crystal on top of the photo of the desired blessing to enhance its effects.

You can also make layers under the candle. For example, a seal of the beatitude, a 3x4 photo of the person, a candle holder and finally the candle that will be used. Place crystals around the candle to amplify the energy at this stage.

There is the option of writing on a circular piece of paper, the person's full name with date of birth, address with zip code, and the requests to be manifested for beatitude. Place the paper (also called a testimony in dowsing) on top of the desired beatitude.

3.° The following steps are for those who will be using olive oil or anointing oils in the candles. Otherwise, skip to step number 4.

3.1° Consecrate the oil to be used with the following prayer:

"I bless you, consecrate you, and give you life, creature of the oil, by its sacred and divine properties attributed to you, by the strength and name of Metatron, prince of the divine presence, by the strength and power of the stars and of this universe, by the strength

and power of mercy, love, peace and redemption and enlightenment to every creature, that everyone who is touched by you may be blessed and enlightened, and have their existence enlightened and all torment ceased, from eternity to eternity, forever and ever, amen."

3.2° Pass the oil over the desired candle while reciting the following prayer:

"I bless you, consecrate you, and give you life, creature of the candle and creature of the fire that will be formed, by this blessed and sacred oil. By the power and name of Metatron, may you travel through all the firmaments of this earth and the heavens, through all the stars, constellations and cosmos of this universe, on all levels, planes, dimensions and physical and spiritual realities. And bring liberation from all pain and suffering to those who receive you. May your strength radiate with your eternal flames, which manifest themselves over all things, and may your light illuminate all darkness, cease all suffering, may your flames warm all cold, and may your blessings radiate eternally, in favor of all those to whom you are offered, in the name of the Divine Creator, forever and ever, from eternity to eternity, by the strength and the name of Metatron, amen".

4.° Light the candle and say the following prayer to the Divine Christ and the desired beatitude:

"I (state your full name), ask for the intercession of the Divine Cosmic Christ, the Divine Planetary Christ, my Higher Self, the Holy Spirit, the Beloved Universe and all my spiritual guides and mentors of light. And I ask that you receive from this candle, this light and this energy, which is consecrated and offered to you. And by this flame that is lit here, and by your grace, love, mercy and power, I ask that this beatitude of Christ be activated in my life (chant the verse of the desired beatitude and its sacred mantra), so that God's divine plan may be realized in my paths. I pray and ask you to (Make your requests), and may it be done, in the name of the Father, the Mother, the Son and the Holy Spirit, amen."

5.° Let the candle burn until the end, and carry on with your day as normal. When the candle has finished burning, store the beatitude seal in a box or container designed to hold your valuable spiritual possessions. A small box is enough to store all the beatitudes that can be used when the need arises.

6.° To activate the beatitudes for other people, simply mention the person's name in the prayer and continue with the activations, consecrating the candle to the person's guides and mentors during the process. Example:

"In the name of (individual's name), I ask for the intercession of the Divine Cosmic Christ, the Divine Planetary Christ, your Higher Self, the Holy Spirit, the Beloved Universe and all the spiritual guides and mentors of light of (individual's name). And I ask that you receive from this candle, this light and this energy, which is consecrated and offered to you. And by this flame that is lit here, and by your grace, love, mercy and power, I ask that this beatitude of Christ be activated in the life of (name of individual), (chant the verse of the desired beatitude and its sacred mantra), so that God's divine plan may be realized in their paths. I pray and ask you to (Make your requests), and may it be done, in the name of the Father, the Mother, the Son, and the Holy Spirit, amen."

The First Beatitude

Blessed are the poor in spirit, because the kingdom of the heavens is theirs."

Matthew 5:3

The First Beatitude

Gospel of Matthew chapter 5:3

"Blessed are the poor in spirit, because the kingdom of the heavens is theirs."

Sacred Mantra: *OM - Ah – Ah – Hah – Kah – Lah - Mah – Hah – Yeh – Shuh – Ah. OM – Yeh – Yah – Chah – Yeh – Mah – Tah – Mah – Yeh – Shuh – Ah.*

Candle color: *White, yellow or gold.*

Crystal: *Citrine and amethyst.*

Of all the things Christ could have said, these are the first words that came out of his lips in the process of channeling the higher worlds, where a beautiful white light descended from the heavens over his head. He was inspired to pass on knowledge to the poor people of his region. In fact, the people of Galilee and the region were suffering from abusive taxes from the emperor Caesar at the time the Beatitudes were spoken. The emperor was relentless, constantly seeking to expand his empire on earth. Many families were lost, creating conflicts between fathers and sons, brothers and sisters, wives and husbands. All this because of small coins that could shape the lives of an entire population. If we pause to reflect, it's no different today, as humanity is still a slave to money and submits to the rules it controls in order to keep everything and everyone in their proper place.

Complaints came from on high about the poverty that was common in his time. The first beatitude, the first message from heaven he received, dealt exactly with the problem everyone faced at the time. For what good are great treasures on earth when we die? When she arrives to receive us, only our evolution, light and clear conscience have the greatest value in the Father's house. All the coins collected throughout our lives are forgotten and passed on to others. Truly I tell you, the riches of the soul are the most valuable and desired things in the entire universe. For everything moves towards the growth of our being. Everyone, in some way, searches deep within for the light that was once lost long ago in their hearts. Even after countless lifetimes, we remember a time when we lived in a world where everything was perfect, in golden grasses, in walls of light, in unparalleled natures. We want to somehow return to this world of light, and for that, we are alive right now, to recover and redeem for what has been lost over time.

When we are in a state of poverty, whether financial, emotional, sentimental, familial, personal, intrapersonal and the like, we lack something. The process of lacking something leads us to try to fill that void. Often, we succeed, sometimes we don't. Consequently, born of an imbalance, the emptiness of the lack grows more and more, leading to addictions of all kinds and attempts to fill the void in our lives with things that have no personal or spiritual value. As long as the cause of the problem remains unresolved, the individual will look for every possible way to quench this pain. Being only a negative root, it can take deep root in our lives, grow and expand, bearing bitter fruit on an endless journey. As long as this root isn't cut, it will still expand underground, creating gaps, holes, wounds and emotional, sentimental, physical, mental and spiritual dependencies on everything that, in some way, has an anesthetic effect on this pain.

The same example is given to the things of heaven, divine things, knowledge and wisdom. Those who are poor in spirit will always seek to fill themselves with light, they will seek to fill themselves with divine wisdom, for this is the greatest wealth of the soul. The endless and incessant search for intimate reform and the evolution of our being is connected to the treasures of heaven, not those of earth. Those who seek to fill the emptiness of existence with experiences not connected to creation will only obtain an illusion about the cessation of their pain. Only God's unconditional love can fill these lives. Only our divine essence can bring the peace we seek, the road we want to travel and the experiences we want to live connected to God's love will always lead us to the longed-for paradise in heaven. Not as a reward for being good, or following the path of light, but as something that is part of the path of those who always seek enlightenment for their souls and their fellow human beings. It is simply a consequence of those who seek unconditional love and make their journeys a constant process of learning and evolution.

As the first beatitude spoken, it opens us up to receive all the next beatitudes of the soul and its infinite journeys between flesh and spirit. When we connect with this word, we tune into the energies that move our being to acquire the treasures of heaven and bring us the wisdom to improve our essence in this incarnation. Becoming more humble, compassionate, removing from us the darkness and imbalances connected to money. This beatitude removes us from the eyes of pride, ego, greed and the control of money over our lives.

New paths are opening up so that we can always stand on a firm and solid foundation. No longer slaves to the coin, but masters over it. This beatitude shows us new paths to follow, where the soul wants to experience so that it can grow and evolve, acquire light and purify itself in all its processes.

All souls wish within themselves to receive love, they wish to live what they committed themselves to before incarnating, in their own life missions. In professions where they wish to exercise their most divine qualities, where their innate talents reverberate to everything and everyone around them. Where they are well recognized, loved, supported and cared for, and can pass on all this love to their fellow human beings. This beatitude connects us with this flow and enables us to see what was once distant or hidden from our eyes.

What would your life be like if you were exactly where your essence wanted to be? Doing exactly what brings you happiness, love and joy? Where you are no longer a slave to money, situations, favors or the *"kindness"* of others? Stop for a few moments and see, your true life is beginning to form here and now, in these words that reach deep inside you and touch your essence right now.

When a soul is connected to their life path, everything flows naturally. Everything harmonizes and becomes new. This is the power of this beatitude, which takes us out of society's control and leads us on a journey in search of eternal knowledge. In the ancient words, it leads us to acquire the treasures of heaven, which are eternal and unimaginably comprehensible to human eyes.

What is the value of a life? What is the value of your peace? What is the value of your evolution? What is the value of your place in heaven? Ask yourself these questions. Since this beatitude is connected to the value of life, to the true value of an incarnation, it shows us everything we value and everything we don't value enough. It doesn't bring poverty, but it does bring the gains of the soul. And simply put, prosperity is a consequence of those who seek and yearn every day to improve their eternal spirits in constant learning, contributing to the world and to themselves in their eternal evolutions. Therein lies the greatest secret of prosperity, for abundance is present in the lives of all those who, in some way, improve the quality of life of the infinite souls who live here. By walking the right path, everything becomes present, everything becomes form, everything becomes real, everything becomes clear, everything becomes goodness and love, everything is healed, everything becomes complete and everything becomes light.

The First Beatitude - Seal

The Second Beatitude

Blessed are those who mourn, because they will be comforted.

Matthew 5:4

The Second Beatitude

Gospel of Matthew chapter 5:4

"Blessed are those who mourn, because they will be comforted."

Sacred Mantra: *OM – Ah – Hah – Kah – Hah – Yah – Yeh – Shuh – Ah. OM – Yeh – Mah – Yeh – Mah – Vah – Yeh – Shuh – Ah.*

Candle color: *White, pink, light blue or gold.*

Crystal: *Rose quartz.*

How many times have we shed tears of sadness in our eyes? How many times have we cried for the pains of life, for the problems we have faced, for the loss of loved ones or for situations that have deeply hurt our being? How many sorrows do we still carry in our hearts from previous lives? How many tears are still waiting to be shed down our cheeks? How many times do we hold back tears so as not to show weakness, only to keep the pain in our chests and hurt ourselves internally? These are profound reflections to be made.

Why does humanity have such a problem showing its feelings? Why do they insist so much on being what they call strong? Where in fact they are only hardening their divine essences and creating hard, empty shells in their souls. The more hardened, rigid and negative a soul is, the more difficulty it has in showing what it feels. Crying is an emotional cleansing of the waters, just as rivers and streams follow their flow to their proper destinations. All of us must also follow the flow of our lives and let everything we feel flow.

We shouldn't harden our souls just to please others. We shouldn't care about the hearts covered in shadows of those who claim and live their lives as sovereigns while hardening their souls with the illusions of this world. Beloved, don't follow these examples. Don't follow what appears to be good. Follow what your soul asks you to follow, what your heart tirelessly asks you to do, to feel, to be. This is the true guidance of the soul, always guided by its highest source, in constant connection with God. The soul knows all things, experiences all things and feels all things. So, my beloved, whatever your heart asks or feels, do it or avoid it, because the heart is the center that connects us with the purest and highest feelings when balanced. The famous *"Touch of God"* in our hearts is simply God telling our soul what to do.

I think of humanity's astonishment when it learns that spirits of light cry, and a lot. The more a spirit shows what it feels, the purer it becomes, because all the movements of its being are allowed to flow with their naturalness and due intensity. They know that it won't do them any good to hold back their tears or squeeze their hearts so that they don't feel what they really feel. This pattern is certainly common and admirable in all spirits who possess light and evolution. Since the universe is made up of constant evolution, this is a reality in every corner of this universe in the dwellings of evolved spirits. In all the worlds of light, everyone shows what they feel, they move their lives and their journeys to be better every day, to be the most perfect versions of themselves, to be the most perfect light. When we reach a point where we decide to become perfect and aim for more light in our lives, and see this light manifest more and more in our paths, from then on, we don't stop, because love and truth become the source of our existence, and at all times we just seek to be perfect in the eyes of the eternal source.

When we open ourselves up to being consoled, consolation is present. You can't console someone who doesn't want to be consoled, or help someone who doesn't ask for help, because that would violate the law of free will. At all times, if we are attentive to listening to the voice of our soul, our guides advise us on our decisions and permissions, on everything that comes in and out of our paths, and based on our choices, they respect what we have decreed for our lives.

This beatitude brings exactly all these words that have been said to each of you. It opens us up to receive the love of heaven, the love that has always been present around us, even with so many blindfolds over our eyes, where we only pay attention to the problems and not the solutions. Love has always been there, by your side, just waiting patiently for a small opportunity to enter your soul and lovingly embrace you for eternity. When we open ourselves up to receive consolation, we also open ourselves up to the energies that bring healing to our pain, healing to our suffering and understanding of what has happened. It is a beatitude of emotional healing, where we can meditate on past sorrows and finally let the tears held in our hearts fall.

Yes, my beloved, emotional healing is one of the great liberations, where that heavy weight on us is finally lifted. And we can move on with our lives, understanding what has passed, healing the wounds of the spirit and continuing on our paths in the divine light. I believe that everyone who reads these sweet words may have some kind of trauma or old pain that still reverberates in their lives. This is so common to humanity, as they persist in running from their feelings and prefer the illusions of the world to the truth of their hearts.

By opening ourselves up to receive the consolation of our soul and our guides, we no longer need to carry the emotional weights on our shoulders, and we can finally let go. In this way, we free ourselves from the unshed tears on our faces, receive healing and the touch of consolation in our hearts, and open ourselves up to a new life.

Where we are no longer bound by past chains, but become new creatures, and everything is renewed. For such is the cycle of all things. This sacred beatitude removes us from melancholic, sad, depressive states, removes the negative from our essence, from our soul, removes the energies and miasmas that promote depressive, dark and sad states. And it opens us up to receive light, consolation and heavenly guidance in our lives.

When we open ourselves up to receive consolation, it can come in many forms, whether through intuition, the sweet words of a friend or family member, or a tenuous dream in which we experience joy or have a helping hand to support us. Remember that Mary's sweet consolation will always be there, and the Virgin Mother's lap will be available to all those who wish it.

The consolation of heaven has always been present through many possible means and ways. We just need to tune in to it. We know for a fact that the light never abandons any soul; there is no rest until everyone is enveloped in the light. None is left behind, knowing that even in your worst moments, there will always be a spiritual guide and mentor by your side. And you will never suffer what you shouldn't, but in truth, you can count on the love of heaven when the tears run down your face, and the pain becomes too much to bear.

The Second Beatitude – Seal

The Third Beatitude

"Blessed are the meek, because they will inherit the earth."

Matthew 5:5

The Third Beatitude

Gospel of Matthew chapter 5:5

"Blessed are the meek, because they will inherit the earth."

Sacred Mantra: OM – Ah – Hah – Kah – Hah – Yeh – Ah – Yeh – Shuh – Ah. OM – Yeh – Mah – Yeh – Hah – Uh – Tzah – Yeh – Shuh – Ah.

Candle color: White, pink or gold.

Crystal: Rose quartz or white quartz.

Inheriting the new Earth is a hot topic these days. Never in the history of our planet has spirituality been so accessible, and streams of information are poured out to seekers every day. The new era is becoming more and more present, and many people are already experiencing what it's like to live in a world in a state of regeneration, as they can easily co-create their own realities.

First of all, we need to understand what the famous planetary transition is and what it means for this world. The planetary transition is a period of change and renewal across the globe. Everything in life is made up of cycles, and naturally our planet, our galaxy and the universe are also made up of increasing cycles towards higher states of vibration and consciousness. We are not separate from these cycles, nor are we separate from our planet. We move and feel these cycles naturally, because our soul is alive and anchored in the material world right now. Just as every spiritual part and its inhabitants are also part of the planet, they also go through these cycles that are completely natural throughout the universe.

Many terrifying theories have been created around this subject, involving supposed timelines of alien intervention, mass destruction, zombie apocalypse, etc. These ideas are formed in the minds of people who lack an understanding of what the planetary transition really means for humanity. The ancients always saw the world through its renewals and always foresaw moments of destruction and renewal on Earth. This was done in antiquity, in the stories told about the famous flood and the planetary renewal movements found in all religions around the world. Unfortunately, this information has been twisted to make people believe that the Earth will be destroyed, that the good souls will ascend and the bad ones will fall into the eternal abyss, creating an apocalyptic narrative of good versus evil and various other tales designed to trap humanity with such tales.

To be honest, perhaps the term *"trap humanity"* isn't exactly the right thing to say. Also, something that has been brought up as a conspiracy theory and somewhat erroneous associations about what the process of incarnating on a school world actually is. Earth is an evolutionary school of the highest difficulty. Here, souls are born to become the best versions of themselves through great trials and atonements.

That said, when they pass away, all souls are taken to the places where they naturally vibrate. If a soul has planted good fruit during its life, it will rest in cities known as spiritual colonies, which are home to all souls who are in the light. If, on death, a soul lived and died in prolonged states far from the light, it will naturally become attuned to places of low vibration, popularly known as the umbral. However, this doesn't necessarily mean that every soul that passes away from the light will tune in to places of darkness. What usually happens is that divine mercy is at work and these souls are taken to spiritual colonies of light. Where they can rest and make amends for their mistakes. From what I've been told, it's only serious cases where souls are pulled away by those who naturally resemble their criminal and low-minded vibrations.

But even then, each case is different and there is no pattern to tell the fate of these individuals. What we can be sure of is that heaven's love and God's mercy will always be there for everyone and everything. It's up to us to choose where to go and where to stay. This information is of great value, as it ends up shattering so many illusions that we may have in this natural process of life, which we will all go through at some point.

The only prison we get into is when our consciential debt gets bigger and heavier in our minds. For lack of knowledge, we choose to reincarnate in endless cycles until we can awaken to the light. And sometimes, this consciential debt that we ourselves feel, leads us on a journey to denser worlds as a form of redemption. This also fits in perfectly with the natural planetary cycles on the planet we live on. When these cycles occur, the world expels everything that no longer vibrates with its planetary energy.

As the Earth is undergoing a renewal, it is not possible to create a new world on a shaky foundation. You can't create the new before the old is destroyed. Unfortunately, we live in a system designed to blind, silence, cover up, divert, deceive and mislead souls onto paths not connected with love. This system has always provided detour and planted seeds that bring bitter fruit and dense roots to the body and mind of humanity as a whole.

If we understand that fear is a tool of control, we will know that if we have to be afraid of something in order to be good, we are under the control of emotion rather than our natural being. If we are good simply because we are good, then we are free to be what our essence is. In this case, we are neither under the domination nor the control of fear, but flow naturally with our soul.

Another point that is very present in our daily lives is the idea that there is only one God on Earth and that everyone should bow down to him. We know, from the knowledge brought by the light, that there are various religions, beliefs, spiritual practices and forms of contact with the spiritual, that, in fact, we have a divine Creator, the principle of all existence, creator of life, light, joy, love, peace, redemption, enlightenment, vivification and all the infinite qualities that good can manifest.

When we think of kings, queens and their thrones raised by empires around the ancient world, we associate a vibrational pattern of sovereignty and control. The act of bowing down to someone greater, whether in status, wealth or material goods, was a common thing in the ancient world. As we assimilate this energy into our soul, which is free and in control of itself, the act of subjugation to someone greater than ourselves is harmful to our spirit. Yet another form of control over our minds. When we bow down, especially to something or someone connected to the opposite plane of light, we give strength, power and permission to be subjugated in flesh and spirit. And when we bow as a sign of love, respect or gratitude to a being of light, then there is no problem and no injury is caused to our soul. As long as everything comes from love, and we feel like doing it, everything is fine.

Although we understand the time and context of the era in which these biblical words were written, where kings and queens certainly ruled over their thrones, we know that the quest for control and power was so great, as was the satisfaction of ruling and being worshipped, that, even today, those same ancient kings and queens, and those who lusted after their thrones and their reigns, find themselves as Dark Lords on infernal and negative levels of spirituality, commanding their servants in search of control, destruction and world sovereignty.

Our financial, political, business and health systems, the agribusinesses (meat industries) that destroy forests to kill more animals, social networks, electronic devices that trap people in content that does nothing to enhance their souls, Wi-Fi networks that are highly toxic to the human body and spirit, uncontrolled consumerism where people consume more than they need and gather materials that are of no use to them, these people accumulate wealth on Earth but forget about the treasures of heaven. Everything around you have been thought up and formed in umbral laboratories as a way of blinding you and distracting you from your path in life. Everything is a way of distracting and separating people.

For the Earth to continue its evolution, there needs to be a transformation, a collapse of all these structures and systems, which are often harmful to spiritual development. Spending a lifetime in a job that brings no fulfillment, getting stuck in routines that cause more harm than good, and repeating the same process every day until the end of our journeys goes completely against love's true plan for this world. The proposal is to leave behind the old laws, to connect with the freedom of being who we are, without judgment, punishment or threats, allowing love to reign in this world. It's a call for a profound transformation, a paradigm shifts in search of an existence more aligned with the divine essence that each human being possesses.

After all, what are the requirements for living in this new world that is appearing on the horizon? The answer is very simple: love. This is the real key to living in happier, purer worlds. For in it we already encompass all the other divine qualities, such as empathy, respect, tolerance, charity, mercy, discernment and wisdom. Dearly beloved, as you have all been told through this medium, only love should reign over your beings. The true light that shines in the heart of the Beloved Christ is simply unconditional love, which does not judge, but respects everyone. Dearly beloved, there is no judgment on the higher planes. There is no raising of the sword to mistreat the less evolved. People may have this idea of medieval wars between light and darkness. But we only leave that for your movies and what you call entertainment.

Make no mistake, the light does defend itself very well. And it doesn't allow itself to be mistreated or subjugated by darkness. The darkness only acts by permission of the light. As tools for the improvement of souls embodied here. They go through trials in order to grow. But it's important to emphasize that the work of the dark only goes as far as each person's free will and personal karma. Both personal and collective. If, by any chance, in a thousandth of a second, the dark forces exceed this limit for whatever reason, they will be instantly removed from action and their plans completely annulled by the light. The light, of course, being of greater vibration, strength and luminosity, can calmly act to put an end to all that inflicts God's will on this world.

This may be shocking information for some. But know that the light cannot interfere with your free will. And if darkness somehow enters your lives, manipulating or carrying out any kind of harmful act to your soul, it's simply because, at some point, you allowed it to happen. Whether through lack of knowledge, inertia, or any action and consequence of your own. Whether that action is conscious or unconscious. Whether it's blindfolding ourselves to situations in front of you, covering your ears so you don't hear what you need to hear, or closing your lips when they need to be opened.

We are not asked to be perfect or to be examples of human beings. Don't fall for the illusions where you are shown perfect lives on social media. These are only temporary illusions that will no longer have a place in this world. A person who loves, who is willing to be better every day and who, even with difficulties, works to improve their essence, already fulfills all the requirements to enter a higher world of consciousness. They don't need to be a religious leader, take various courses in spirituality, have contact with spirits and extraterrestrials, be a millionaire donor to needy causes, have a religion or belong to a specific religious movement, or even be someone who shows themselves to be charitable on glass screens. Even the neediest living being with basic needs can be much more evolved than those who have everything but lack the wisdom of the soul. For if this needy being vibrates in love and is moved by it, even in the face of all life's difficulties, then this is the kingdom of heaven. And on the new Earth, he will surely live.

God sees men's hearts as they really are. He knows their burdens, their faults, their successes and their mistakes. He knows what they suffer and what they rise to. You see, it doesn't take much to evolve, just willingness and desire. When a soul wants, it seeks, it goes after, it does whatever is within its reach and often out of its hands, to achieve what it desires. It wants to be better, not to live in a happy world, but simply to be what it is. Those who vibrate in love don't vibrate because they expect to receive something in return. You don't do good to earn good deeds or spiritual points. But you vibrate in love because it is majestic and as a result you bring and feel happiness, joy and satisfaction from it.

Let's not forget that the process of planetary exile is not formed by a vengeful arm, nor by harsh beings who cast souls in need of evolution onto the earth. This whole process is only carried out by the unconditional love and consciential choice of each soul. Every individual, at every moment, is always supported by beings of light, where there is no judgment and no crooked looks. Everyone, at every moment, is embraced by unconditional love, everyone is completely supported in love, loved in pure love, every second, without any distinction.

I ask you to change your mindset if you think that the process of exile is formed by low qualities of the spirit's maturity. This is a big mistake, because all light only loves and respects the decisions made by everyone and everything. And it waits anxiously for the briefest moment to be able to pour out its radiations of unconditional love on those who walk difficult paths in life and death. Everything is an opportunity for evolution, everything is an opportunity for growth. Exile is not a sentence of death, suffering and pain, but just another path in love, given by the divine Creator. If they were to remain on this Earth, which will gradually increase in vibration as it approaches its regenerative state, their spirits would be completely crushed by the high vibration. Causing much greater pain than the process of planetary exile.

Those who are light do not rejoice in the suffering and pain of those who have lived away from their essence, but only wait for the right moment to love, care for and support them. And this is how it is done on all the higher levels of consciousness, where love reigns and will always reign.

Now that we've touched on the inheritance of souls on Earth, let's go back a little to the meaning of the biblical verse of this beatitude. Meekness, the form of non-reaction to aggressive situations that can take us away from our essence. Meekness, like love, is always present in all spirits who possess light. Light, dear friends, does not respond in the same vibratory range as darkness. If darkness promotes chaos, light promotes peace. If darkness promotes discord, anger and fighting, light promotes gentleness, forgiveness and love.

When Christ gave this message, the earth was in a state of energy where an eye for an eye and a tooth for a tooth was the law of peoples and nations. And for many centuries this was the case, where people resolved their conflicts and threats through the sword and death. And of course, enlightened people were seen as holy, where a gentleness was seen by everyone around. The meek were signs of enlightenment, sanctified souls who had come into the world to bring about great changes in our world. Always with their missions where peace reigned, and in their hearts devotion to the Most High was greater and more present than the anger that reigned over the nations. When these souls set a good example, the light was awakened in the consciences of those who, lost in the world, only reproduced what they saw every day in their lives. Do you realize that, even when we are involved in conflicting situations, Christ and high spirituality ask us to be meek. This raises our vibrational frequency and brings more light into our being. Reality changes in our favor. And this change is felt by everyone in our being, the motivation to be pure and true like love is an energy that spreads easily, like a great inspiration to awaken in us sparks, flames and fires of devotion to the Creator, always through the fullest, most peaceful, tenuous and perfect love. Full of love and mercy, qualities that all saints possess.

This beatitude comes precisely to bring us that. The peace of gentleness over our bodies, over our lives, situations, desires, hopes, dreams, achievements, paths, relationships, family and wherever else it may arise. It promotes calm, serenity, and teaches us to be more peaceful with others, more tolerant, kinder and more receptive to the situations and people around us. It also promotes, according to each person's openness, the qualities necessary for the evolution of our being, through the Christic energies of unconditional love.

Being connected to Earth's inheritance, it shows us why our paths are taken to a denser planet. It reveals our past faults and how to correct them in order to be better every day. To do this, try meditating on the subject and be open to receiving the intuition that may come into your soul from your higher self. This beatitude also triggers a healing process which, if practiced with dedication, can help to heal the deepest wounds of our former planetary exile from Capela, and helps us to understand the past and accept our old mistakes with love and gentleness.

The Third Beatitude – Seal

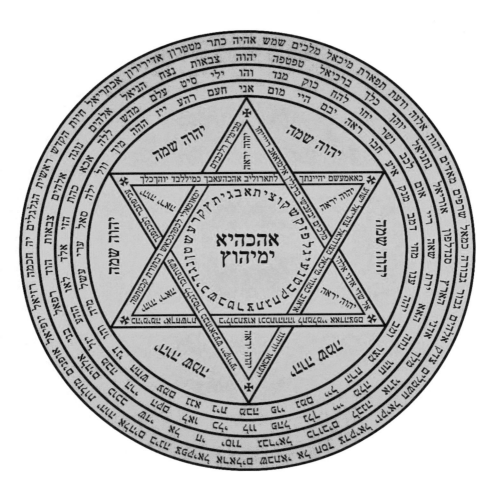

The Fourth Beatitude

"Blessed are those who hunger and thirst for righteousness, because they will be filled."

Matthew 5:6

The Fourth Beatitude

Gospel of Matthew chapter 5:6

"Blessed are those who hunger and thirst for righteousness, because they will be filled."

Sacred Mantra: *OM – Ah – Hah – Vah – Leh – Kah – Hah – Yeh – Yeh – Shuh – Ah. OM – Yeh – Mah – Mah – Hah – Yeh – Mah – Vah – Yeh – Shuh – Ah.*

Candle color: *White, yellow, dark blue or gold.*

Crystal: *Citrine.*

Ah, if we were to talk about all the injustices in this world, we would spend countless pages addressing such a deep and complex subject, where many don't see all the hidden triggers that led to their conclusions. First of all, we need to recognize that we are imperfect beings, but that we are no less worthy of divine mercy.

Sometimes we get it right, sometimes we get it wrong, sometimes we get it right more than we get it wrong and vice versa. What really determines our path is the choices we make in life. It is, in fact, a complicated subject to tackle, because a large part of humanity is not prepared to understand that many things that happen in their lives are just the result of their own decisions, their own infamous karma, just ways chosen by the soul to alleviate the consciential guilt of its actions.

In an imperfect way, of course, because it is not necessary to suffer in order to be at peace with our conscience. There is no longer any need for this in this world, or rather, there never was.

We incarnate forgetting our past lives, unaware of our actions in other lives. This is an act of divine mercy, as knowing all our previous failings would make this life too difficult to follow. Every life is an opportunity for evolution, and I don't wish to enter the cycle of Samsara by living to pay for past mistakes. I wish to bring the knowledge to release it from us, without any more suffering or debts to pay.

All mistakes are part of our learning process, and we should only and exclusively look at them with love and gratitude. Because through them we can learn the lessons we need to evolve morally and spiritually. On the one hand, we are motivated for our own good to understand the consequences of our mistakes, whether made in the past or the present, as a way of improving our being and understanding that everything we do, whether for good or evil, does have a consequence. However, in the planes of light, there is no God, judge or tribunal to point out our faults, only our own conscience, which at one time or another awakens to continue its journey towards the light.

This beatitude is particularly effective for people who feel wronged in life, who live difficult paths and realities, where nothing seems to work out and there is always a problem to be faced. When something is solved, something else comes along to continue the vicious cycle of pain. Something real needs to happen, something tangible that shows that this cycle needs to end. That's the power of this beatitude, where internal and external changes are provoked so that God's justice can be fully manifested in our lives. With the Creator's justice on our side, all situations seem to resolve themselves and come to an end in accordance with God's highest law.

This beatitude enables people to understand their faults and resolve conflicts in the face of life's injustices. Normally, certain patterns repeat themselves in a soul's life as a persistent lesson to be learned. Until it is solved, the pattern repeats itself indefinitely. These patterns or vicious cycles need to be broken. Just as in justice, redemption is needed for evil to cease. Without redemption for actions taken in the past, it is not possible to move forward, because the same energies and consequences will still manifest on our paths. When we talk about redemption, we are talking about acts, actions and significant changes that promote restitution for the mistakes, regrets and pain caused. When this properly manifests, all negative cycles come to a true end. As you work and meditate on this beatitude, pay close attention to your intuition, your visions and the advice you receive. See what the cause of your persecutions is and how you can properly end them in God's love.

When we talk about justice, we're talking about a spiritual force that in human eyes is implacable, but in the eyes of spirituality is something focused on love and mercy. With it, we can obtain strong energetic protection with divine justice, but know that this justice is full of gentleness and always focused on love. Humanity tends to look to God to satisfy its desire for revenge, claiming that it is right to make those who made them suffer, suffer. But nothing is so superfluous as this in the eyes of those who can see everything.

All spirits connected to this vibration naturally vibrate in love and mercy, because this is God's true justice, an endless mercy. Knowing this, we must realize that if certain unjust situations present themselves in our lives, it is because of something hidden that is collapsing this energy in our lives. There is always a reason for certain events on our paths, but that doesn't mean that we have to suffer in order to pay off debts known or unknown to us.

A small example that spirituality wants to give us is the following: imagine that in a past life, a couple was separated by marriage contracts between families. A girl's heart was already wrapped in love for a young man. However, forced by her family to fulfill their contracts as part of her father's business, she was given in marriage to a stranger, for whom she has no feelings. In this case, to whom, in God's eyes, is the proper love union owed? To the one promised in marriage via a family union, or to the young man for whom the girl has her heart full of love?

Let's say that the young man who truly loves the girl is murdered by the husband promised to the woman. Out of jealousy, envy, anger, possession and feelings not connected to love. The girl goes on to live in an unenlightened relationship, where she only serves to satisfy the desires of her husband, who has no virtuous feelings towards her.

In another life, these souls incarnate again and spirituality brings everyone together to settle their past debts. The husband, promised to the wife by a family union, and the girl meet again and start living a common relationship with promises of engagement, but without any great virtues or expectations on either side. As times have changed, feelings can be milder or more intense, depending on the case. Influenced by the current society of their incarnations, they are influenced to get engaged and married in order to achieve financial stability, a vampiric relationship focused on the comfort of having someone by their side to satisfy their more carnal desires in terms of the economy, finances and simple earthly pleasures.

Realize that, even in this new life, the issue of marrying for money again manifests itself, this time not related to the father's business as it once was. But the energy still reverberates in the souls of both in this case, connected internally in their beings and by the external influence of family and friends around them. However, by the movement of fate and by the will of God, that young man who had a real feeling for the girl incarnates at the same time as she is alive.

With a move of the universe, the light guides, God and all of life conspire so that the two can meet. Even through the influence of fate, they both meet, he is single, she is promised to marry her fiancé. But, as love cannot be extinguished, nor can it be forgotten, when the two begin to get to know each other, and even at the first glance, they know that something different springs up in their hearts. The girl then begins to nurture more real and subtle feelings for the young man, who responds in the same way to her. True love begins to take shape in their hearts.

The girl then, with a strong desire to love the young man, decides to separate from her fiancé and start living with her true love. The groom's life then falls apart, because his home with her was not built on solid rock, but on shifting sands that could easily be blown away by the wind, picked up by the sea and erased by the time.

If you were that groom, unaware of spirituality and of these words I'm saying to each of you, would you feel wronged? Betrayed? Forsaken by God? Would you look for every way to get your wife back? Gifts, money, cars, houses, sex, flowers, countless promises and dreams to be fulfilled? Would they seek a spiritual hand to sweeten, bind, hold and keep the bride by your side? Would you do or ask for spells works for destructions of enemies, death and seek out dark magicians to end a life in the same way you may have ended one in another life?

We realize that justice can be much more impartial than we ever imagine. It is a completely fair way of harmonizing what is out of balance. If we think about it, how many similar people and situations can we name right now? How many conversations, stories and events completely similar to this tale happen in our daily lives?

We realize that God's divine justice may go far beyond what our eyes can comprehend, but it is by no means a decree of endless suffering.

Because of the countless examples we can give, be very careful when you act in the name of justice in your ways. I believe that is the message I wish to convey here in these pages. Justice here will not hurt, because this beatitude is totally focused on the good and the light. However, it has a strong arm and can apply its punishments if unjust situations occur in the lives of its practitioners.

Therefore, by practicing it, you'll understand that you can't run away from your mistakes and you won't be a victim anymore. But you will look for solutions so that you can finally be at peace with the situations around you. How wonderful it would be if the citizens of Earth stopped looking for the guilty in their lives and looked for what would raise them up to solve their problems. Looking for blame, dear ones, is a movement of the ego of your beings, where it always seeks to blame something or someone for the events generated by your own actions.

This beatitude brings justice to your paths, it fills you with energies and forces that bring order and law to your ways, to your lives. It brings unjust situations to an end, and the innocent can triumph in the face of life's battles. It can be used in legal cases where God's law needs to be manifested above the judgments of men. All aspects connected to justice, its energies, laws, courts, sentences and so on are governed by this beatitude. It can be used as a way of connecting with the divine. And above all, when you need to call on God's justice to overcome the persecutions of this world, that's where it really shines and becomes complete in the eyes of the Creator. It also provides an understanding of your harvest and why your positive and negative actions reverberate throughout your life. We even find intuitions and, often, revelations of the roots of our current ills in distant times briefly forgotten for a lifetime. Events that could always be solved if only we would stop running from them.

The energy of justice always shines incorruptibly throughout the cosmos, being an existential factor of God. It is always present in everything and everyone. At all times, it is a force that can be freely accessed to ask for its help in our daily struggles. And this is what we must do, because we must never allow the blows of life to flow freely into our spirit. The more we allow it, the more we will suffer. But the more we fight to overcome them, the more we will be filled with the glorious victory over evil. This is how justice manifests itself throughout the world, it's belongs to those who move and walk with her. Remember this and be filled with this wonderful white light with yellow tones that will fill you for ever and ever.

An important factor in this beatitude is that it brings us closer to the forces of Jupiter, the Father, and the energetic qualities of this great planetary being. Where his forces are manifested on our paths and we can receive his help on our journeys in this life. It is also great for repelling people, spirits and intrusive forces who are in debt to their consciences and who run afoul of the law of man and God. Since it is manifest over everything, nothing can prevail before it.

The Fourth Beatitude - Seal

The Fifth Beatitude

"Blessed are the merciful,
because they will obtain mercy."

Matthew 5:7

The Fifth Beatitude

Gospel of Matthew chapter 5:7

"Blessed are the merciful, because they will obtain mercy".

Sacred Mantra: *OM - Ah – Hah – Veh – Lah – Kah – Hah – Yah – Yeh – Shuh – Ah. OM – Yeh – Mah – Mah – Hah – Yeh – Mah – Vah – Yeh – Shuh – Ah.*

Candle color: *White, pink or gold.*

Crystal: *Rose quartz.*

To speak of mercy, yes... I take a few breaths and its primordial source immediately comes to mind: unconditional love. Love and mercy go hand to hand; mercy is nothing more than the beautiful fruit of love, which is more enlightened and regenerated than we know in this world. The fruit of which all the heavenly spirits know and consume daily.

What do we understand by mercy? Is it the fruit of compassion for our fellow human beings? We see the mercy of the divine creator on Earth every day. Where every enlightened soul, who shares mercy and lives it in their days, is never alone and helpless. We realize that all those who live their journeys for the greater good of their souls as well as for the collective, are always supported by a greater force.

All those who are merciful will achieve mercy. For those who vibrate in love achieve love, those who vibrate in light achieve light, those who vibrate in fraternity achieve fraternity. We could give endless examples of how love brings love and how mercy brings mercy. But this verse in particular speaks of something that many may not be able to understand because they only see what is said over the surface.

When the beloved Yeshua Hamashiach uttered this beatitude, he was already connecting with the aspect of forgiveness for souls in need of light and evolution. Practicing mercy means acquiring the removal of past guilt, faults, pain and mistakes. Is one of the most beautiful and powerful ways of making reparation to our souls for the past mistakes we have made on our journey. When we are merciful, someone will be merciful to us. We don't practice mercy in search of spiritual rewards or favors, we practice mercy because it's in our true essence to be only light. Let love be pure and true, the fruit of all the good things in this world. We have chosen the path of this love, and naturally this love will heal our wounds. The universe will place all the necessary situations, people, guides and paths in our path so that we can always climb a little higher on our evolutionary journey.

I think it's too simple just to say that those who are merciful will also receive mercy in their lives. The word itself already carries within it many great things for the spirit that have never been mentioned, but all souls feel. Just by connecting with the word, we can already feel its white, rainbow-colored radiance in our lives. It's as if we feel God embracing us with all his love. It's like feeling the embrace of life. And for that, we have no words in our vocabulary to describe in the small words contained here. He who achieves mercy achieves brotherhood and universal love. Those who practice mercy are always renewed. He who lives mercy lives in God. And whoever lives in God lives in full divine love. And nothing else exists beyond that.

To talk about divine mercy is to talk about God. Since God is the primary and universal source of all love and mercy, he will never leave his sons and daughters abandoned. God has compassion for all of us at every moment, every second of our lives. He longs and desires for us all to be able to come together, to live in peace, in harmony, without any more wars or conflicts. He wants all those who are lost to find a way and achieve the redemption of their souls. No matter who they are or what they have done, there is forgiveness for everything. For the divine source is forgiveness and unconditional love with no barriers and no limits. Where there are no judgments, crooked looks or anger that only hurts and does not enhance life. Since life is an existential factor for God, he wants everyone to be able to live. And not just survive. He wants everyone to be able to feel life at every moment, every second of their existences. He wants everyone to be able to be light, see light and feel light in their hearts at every moment.

Regardless of your past actions, God extends his hand to heal and forgive. Just like us, we have the free will to plant and harvest. Even if our planting wasn't the best, God gives us the choice to renew our planting and start again. So that once again, we can be aligned with the light, which will only bring us love and joy. Too often, we choose to move away from this light through wrong choices that will only bring us bitter fruit on our paths. God, being pure love and mercy, the universe being a source of infinite love, places situations around us in the hope that we will wake up to all the actions that go against our existential plan, which is only to be light.

Mercy is still present in all souls, even those who wander and wish to separate themselves from their creative sources of light, even in moments of painful learning chosen by our own conscience. As I write these words, I have a clear vision of a poor, homeless man, barefoot on a cold floor; in his eyes, a distant vision of happiness, where he longs for a plate of food. And next to him, I see a spirit of light, his mentor, constantly supporting him so that he no longer suffers the hardships of his incarnation. We don't know who this resident is or was, but it doesn't matter, because love is for everyone. This resident, although not seen by society, is seen by God, by spirituality, by his guides and brothers and sisters. And every night, he goes to astral homes, where he receives food, a bath, clean clothes and leisure. We don't know the events, choices and paths that led this man to be in this situation, but we do know that, despite everything, the loving eyes of the Creator will not be closed to him.

The same can be said for all those who remain in the darkness of their minds, where they act against the plan of light. Even the worst of men, as considered by mankind, can receive divine mercy. There is no "sin" without forgiveness, there is no mistake that cannot be corrected, there is no fall that cannot be recovered or ascended towards heaven. Everything is based on our personal choices, whether to remain in the state we're in or to get back on our feet and look for new directions in life. Truly know that even the most negative spirit, from the moment it sincerely asks for help, will be instantly supported by the forces of light and will begin a new journey in his existence.

The vision of the famous hell really doesn't match the reality of the spiritual planes. Fallen angels, demons or any kind of earthly denomination that humanity has given to less enlightened spirits of love. Everyone can be helped, but only when they allow it. Therein lies the mercy of the divine creator, which is given in the most perfect abundance and love to all. At every moment, it has always been present and will always be present for those who ask for it. The essence of mercy is the basis of love and forgiveness, in understanding the actions and reactions of ourselves and our fellow human beings. Just knowing that every wound caused, every pain felt, every aggression in life is just old roots that have not been healed. To achieve mercy is to be God on Earth. And to be God on Earth is to spread his love to the four corners of this world.

Mother Holy Mary is the closest example I have when it comes to mercy. Many times, the opposite plane sends its slaves and dark entities to do its bidding. And she, who is very wise, knows that they are only spirits without the light of knowledge, and that they have total freedom to free themselves and get out of their suffering, all they have to do is ask. However, they choose to remain in that state, because they don't know that they are where they are by choice and not because they are bound to their dark masters. Only if they receive light, or awaken their essence, can they ask and they will be promptly answered by divine mercy.

For me, Mother Holy Mary is synonymous with mercy and love. I faithfully believe that she imbues these qualities, being herself a manifestation of this energy in this world. An archetype of mercy, love and the redemption of souls. I've been able to feel and tune in to her and I've even had the opportunity to feel what she feels. Truly, her evolution, love, empathy and mercy are indescribable. I could feel myself completely enveloped in her bonds of love, and it seemed to me that I had evolved hundreds of years in a few seconds in these brief, serene moments. The source of love was tremendous. Now, after feeling and being as she is, I could see why she is such a kind and merciful figure in our world.

This beatitude is used to manifest mercy in every aspect of our existence. Through it, we can be more compassionate, tolerant, kind, understandable, patient, acquire empathy, love, light, forgiveness, wisdom and all the fruits of the Holy Spirit. It is used to support, care for, protect, deliver, heal, liberate, ascend, enlighten and pacify everything and everyone. It also promotes the connection with merciful forces, such as Mary, saints, angels and spirits whose faces and manifestations vibrate at this loving frequency. We can also promote the energies of mercy for people, spirits, situations, timelines, the past, present and future, our planet and even other planetary spheres. One example that comes to mind is Mother Mary's call for everyone to send the light of this beatitude to the valley of the crucified, which are places on the spiritual realms where there are many souls reliving the crucifixion process, where many souls remain to this day because of this terrible practice carried out in the ancient times of our civilization.

"Being the virtue of all saints and angels. Mercy is the fruit from which all pure souls will be able to reap on the day of their judgments." - Ars Aurora - A Guide of Light.

Try sending this energy to the planet every day, and you'll know that you'll be promoting a great light in the lives of all humanity. And remember: *"Blessed are the merciful, for they shall obtain mercy."*

Matthew 5:7

The Fifth Beatitude - Seal

The Sixth Beatitude

"Blessed are the pure in heart because they will see God."

Matthew 5:8

The Sixth Beatitude

Gospel of Matthew chapter 5:8

"Blessed are the pure heart, because they will see God."

Sacred Mantra: *OM – Ah – Vah – Lah – Kah – Heh – Yah – Ah – Hah – Yeh – Shuh – Ah. OM – Yeh – Yah – Vah – Yah – Mah – Vah – Tah – Mah – Yeh – Shuh – Ah.*

Candle color: *White or gold.*

Crystal: *White quartz.*

Here we have a mystery that humanity has not yet understood. Only the clean of heart will see God, because God is in all the good things around us. You can't ascend to the highest heavens without first being cleansed of your inner imperfections and guilt. They will naturally pull your soul further and further into the abyss. And make no mistake, the abyss I'm referring to is always the abyss of consciousness, where you can only see the darkness projected by your own actions and the consequences that yourself have projected onto your life.

When the soul falls, it enters a dark and lightless vibratory state. The soul is enveloped by darkness and vibrations that we can call *"dirty"* due to the energetic and vibrational levels that spread through their vibratory field. When a soul is in this state, it cannot rise to more subtle and luminous vibratory levels, because its current frequency makes it impossible for it to reach the planes of light peacefully. This often results in the soul being wounded by such a vibration that its spirit cannot withstand the natural energies of light. This difficulty in receiving light applies to those who choose to remain in darkness, rather than those who seek to improve their spirits and their lives. With each step, they can cleanse themselves of their inner darkness and access the most luminous and beautiful places in spirituality. It's important to mention that this factor doesn't apply to spiritual rescues, because even the most negative of beings can be supported by guides and beings of light and taken to spiritual colonies that best suit their current state, so that they can begin the process of healing their souls.

Since God is the most beautiful and pure form we know, there is no such thing as sin, guilt, darkness or any other name that the Earth and its inhabitants can give him. The balance between light and darkness has never been about being connected to God and, at the same time, working with the dark forces that, by choice and their own knowledge, choose to act against the plans of the light. In God, the source of light, there are no shadows, darkness or gloom. He is a great sun, who, in his perfection, only illuminates, magnifies, elevates and loves. The fall of darkness is, yes, a way for God to show the consequences of your mistakes in your own life, but it doesn't mean that he sympathizes or aligns himself with those actions.

Because everything that binds, ties up, weakens, everything that brings pain, guilt or fear, certainly doesn't come from God. And many times, consciously or unconsciously, we choose to remain in states that are not connected to the creative source. In these states, we have great difficulty accessing God, because our own actions pull us down, while God's actions only raise us up. When we are aware that something needs to be changed in our lives, and for some reason we put it aside, whether because of fear, insecurity, fear of changes, possible internal and external disturbances on our paths, we are giving clear and precise permission for disharmony to continue to be active in our lives. As tiring as it may seem, having to resolve all the things that come our way is necessary if we are to free ourselves from all the darkness of our past.

All these situations are tests and lessons that need to be resolved in our existence. And many of them derive from our past lives and them repeated endlessly until they are resolved. Think of them as a teaching for the purification of the soul by a crystalline white flame, making total reference to the white ray of the Great Brotherhood of Light, all these teachings given to us are just forms of divine mercy, in promoting those situations to be resolved, and free our souls from these timeless bonds.

The teachings were never painful, it was never the aim to bring pain in order to evolve. People associate the lessons of Serapis Bey, the master of the white ray, as expiations of the soul and hard teachings to follow, but in reality, they are so gentle and peaceful for all those who wish to learn. What actually brought the pain was only the pain itself, holding on with all its might to not be removed; the purpose is simply to let go and release from our hands those heavy ropes that hurt us so much. It is to extinguish that hot ember in our chest, to tranquilize our soul and consciously choose to no longer vibrate and to no longer insist on the paths of darkness.

Sometimes guides and mentors influence certain events so that we can resolve them in our lives. As we live on a school planet, tests are given and it's up to us to answer them. The guides and mentors are there to teach, support and instruct their students, and with all their hearts, all teachers want to see their students walking on their own two feet. For too much support does not bring evolution to anyone. And if the soul, aware of this, still chooses to remain in those states of darkness, inertia or contentment. Does not work on these aspects in their life, or worse, chooses to ignore them, they will consequently be going against the perfect life that God provides for them. Do you understand how simple it is? When a soul seeks the purity of its life, and searches with all its heart for the source of eternal life, then that same source will place in your path all the infinite possibilities for finding him. In such a simple but beautiful way, God makes himself present to everyone at all times, even in those situations where we see no way out, we feel something, a greater and more divine force supporting us and telling us that everything will be fine. Can you recognize God in these moments? Do you recognize God now in your life? Can you see God in purity?

God, a sun without limits, whose rays are the most powerful light a soul that we can feel, can only be accessed by those who choose to see him in his most perfect purity, without the infinite earthly archetypes and their forms that his face has been molded into over the aeons of time. Therefore, only those with a pure heart will be able to see God. If there is still any guilt, weight or remorse inside you, you will still be trapped in the illusory chains of darkness. Likewise, when, overcome by shame and remorse, we instinctively look away from God, because we don't want the light to see us in shameful states. Humanity tends to not show weakness, and to take matters into their own hands, resisting all afflictions as much as possible in order to demonstrate strength and power. But little do they know that they are in negative behavior, because they end up hurting their souls and their essence by not seeking help, and even if unconsciously, knowing that they cannot solve their afflictions alone, they end up breaking themselves, thinking that they are showing strength, in fact, they are showing weakness. And they break down more and more by once again allowing these situations to spread through their lives.

At all times in our lives, we avoid showing our weaknesses, mistakes and regrets to other people. Whether it's work, family, wife or husband, children or relatives, we always want to show that we're fine and that nothing is bothering us at the moment. By ego, we always want to show ourselves that we're living the best life possible, and when we see someone in a better situation than us, we don't want to show our current state of life, either out of shame or fear of judgment. From this same shame, we have the energy that encompasses all those distorted feelings that distance us from the eyes of the Creator. As long as anything not connected to the light resides in our chest, we won't be able to see the most perfect light in our lives. The light it will always be at our side, make no mistake about that, but living in it, in truth and love, is only for those who, in their greater will, wish to find love and the deepest redemption that exists in this universe, unconditional love.

Knowing then, that we need to be pure in our hearts to see God, without malice, shame, guilt, fear, impure desires, and begin to recognize God in the little things, in the little joys, in the little smiles, in the sweet breezes of the wind, in the tenuous blue of the skies, in the sweet songs of the birds, in the pure smell of nature, in feeling the touch of the earth on our feet, in the sweet embrace of the skies, in the calm of the moon, in the enchantment of the night, in the brilliance of the stars, in the sound of the waves of the sea, in the singing of the birds of a new day, in the beauty of nature and its infinite forms of life, in the birth of a new sprout, in the sweet honey of the bees, in the sweet perfume of the flowers and in the dawn of a new day, God is so present in all these moments, of such beauty, of such goodness, of such love, it is enough for us to recognize him in the small pleasures of life. Because life itself is the most perfect manifestation of God, all we have to do is recognize it.

God, my dear brothers and sisters, is the source of life, and we only access God when we truly live. Then we see God at every moment, with every sigh, every smile, every tear, every love. Among infinite possibilities, there are infinite manifestations. God is present, you just have to be able to recognize him.

This beatitude, given to us by our Beloved Brother Yeshua, teaches us that we must be clean in our essence in order to access the source of creation. We cannot rise without first ridding ourselves of everything that keeps us stuck in the past or in the darkness of now. Darkness cannot access the light in its high heavens, but God can access darkness in its deepest abyss. By meditating on this verse, chanting its mantra and meditating on its sacred seal, we can gain insights into all the darkness, shadows, guilt, regret, anger and imbalances that need to be worked through and faced by us. It can also promote the cleansing of these past energies in order to free our soul from the pain that is so deeply rooted in our heart. When it is properly cleansed, then we will be able to see God in his most perfect fullness. This beatitude is a divine word that we can use to access God, cleanse our hearts and intimately seek the luminous paths of love. For without love, nothing will be done.

The Sixth Beatitude - Seal

The Seventh Beatitude

"Blessed are the peacemakers, because they will be called sons of God."

Matthew 5:9

The Seventh Beatitude

Gospel of Matthew chapter 5:9

"Blessed are the peacemakers, because they will be called sons of God."

Sacred Mantra: *OM – Ah – Rah – Shah – Keh – Vah – Ah – Yeh – Lah – Yeh – Shuh – Ah. OM – Yeh – Yah – Mah – Yeh – Yah – Mah – Ah – Mah – Yeh – Shuh – Ah.*

Candle color: *White or gold.*

Crystal: *White quartz.*

When we think of a perfect world, where only joy, peace, love and infinite goodness and divine plenitude reign, nothing ever crosses our minds that is contrary or even offensive to this image. Perhaps even a memory from our past, but that doesn't fit here at the moment.

Peacemakers are all those who, in their lives, in their ways, in their words and in the depths of their hearts, bring the light of the Creator to every corner of this world. They are those who radiate divine love in their auras and heal those who approach them. It is the sincere heart willing to help, it is the heart broken in God's love. It is the dwelling place of the Holy Spirit and where Christ is present on their paths, guiding them at all times to always be the divine love and light that has always existed in their hearts.

On the higher planes of spirituality, home to completely beneficial spirits and bearers of God's love, they only aim to bring this love to every corner of this universe. They truly seek to illuminate every dark particle in pure light. As previously mentioned, God, the divine and infinite sun, sends his light in the form of his children, who promote his love and peace wherever they go. His love and light take forms throughout the world, their forms take other forms and they access every living creature on this planet. It's all just a way of accessing and getting in touch with those souls who need his warmth so, so much.

Just as in the highest spheres of light, beloved spirits enveloped in love decide to incarnate to help humanity. In this incarnation, they promote peace, love and light. In the end, they are called children of God. For Christ already knew about these missionary souls who came here to bring about the most profound revolutions, break paradigms and bring love in its purest form to every corner of this world. Remember that you don't have to be a missionary with a thunderous mission on Earth, but just be the light that you already are but have forgotten over the ages. In this way, you too are called a child of God. The missionary mission was just a small example to give, because all those who spread love, peace, fraternity and the divine virtues of the sacred primordial source are also called children of God. Every light matters in this world, every particle of goodness emanating here can bring about profound revolutions on this planet. I believe this, I know that love brings love, and I know that light brings light. For this reason, I also know that all our efforts to bring this light will surely be rewarded with more light and love on our paths and also on this beloved planet Earth.

We need to live our lives as a way of leaving a spiritual legacy to all future souls. To leave a beautiful example to be given to all those who seek the knowledge that we have mastered. That's why we need to find ways to eternalize our light here on this plane. Whether it's through wise words that echo in the deepest depths of our listeners' being, or through concrete actions that can change lives, or simply by being the infinite goodness and light that we have always been. In this way, by manifesting the eternal light on this planet, we are also eternalized by God the Father and Mother in heaven.

Have you ever stopped to ask yourselves if your actions today contribute in any way to the life of society? Have you asked yourself if you are living what you came to live and accomplish on this Earth? Do our lives really need to be monotonous on a gray scale? Waking up, working, eating, sleeping and repeating the process until our last breath? We know deep down that our lives don't have to be this way. We are developing a planetary consciousness that teaches us that we must live what God instructed us to before our incarnation. We know that, in the perfect planes of spirituality, of the angels and mentors of light, our path is always filled with happiness, growth, learning, evolution, where we can always rest in peaceful green pastures, adorned with colorful flowers, camellias, sunflowers and all natural beauty.

To be a missionary is to bring light to the world. It's being a vehicle of light for all those who come to us. It's being able to make a difference in people's lives. It's being that person on whom everyone can rely in their moments of distress. To be a missionary is to be the divine spirit who works tirelessly for internal and external improvement. Improving themselves and society as a whole through their actions. This word shows us our role in this world and how we can contribute to planetary evolution and ascension as a whole. It shows us the paths to be taken and teaches us step by step how we can be the differentiating factor, the sacred key that will open doors for the infinite light of the Creator to manifest more and more on this planet. By meditating on this sacred verse, we can also obtain God's peace and learn how to keep it in our lives, also freeing us from crooked paths and situations that can lead us away from the divine soul of the Creator.

Peace, one of the most beautiful and divine forms of God, is the tranquility and harmony manifested in the little things in our lives. It is the most complete fraternity between people, it is the song of birds on a radiant morning. It's the sound of the waters in such tranquil and infinite sources of creation. It's the sun that warms, the rain that wets and purifies, it's the sweet night and its warmth and serenity. It's the feeling of overcoming a mountain and looking at the view from the top. It's a mother's love and a father's wisdom. Peace, my brothers and sisters, is the Source in its most beautiful perfection.

The Seventh Beatitude - Seal

The Eighth Beatitude

"Blessed are those who have been persecuted because of righteousness, because the kingdom of the heavens is theirs."

Matthew 5:10

The Eighth Beatitude

Gospel of Matthew chapter 5:10

"Blessed are those who have been persecuted because of righteousness, because the kingdom of the heavens is theirs."

Sacred Mantra: *OM – Ah – Heh – Vah – Heh – Kah – Lah – Mah – Hah – Yeh – Shuh – Ah. OM – Yeh – Mah – Lah – Hah – Yeh – Mah – Tah – Mah – Yeh – Shuh – Ah.*

Candle color: *White, yellow, dark blue or gold.*

Crystal: *Citrine.*

I wondered for a few moments what this word of Jesus meant. What did he mean by those who are persecuted for righteousness' sake? A term that can be all-encompassing and address aspects that, from the outside, seem superficial, but are, in fact, profound because of the wisdom passed down.

When we talk about persecution for the sake of justice, we are talking about the persecution of the light in this world. As justice is referred to in one of its meanings, it is the justice of God, it is the Christ energy, it is the force of eternal goodness being manifested in this world. It is the word of the Creator, unconditional love, and all its bearers of the sacred light of this world, this is the justice brought by heaven to earth. Which will naturally raise up all those who run from it, or who are against its coming into this world. This verse is very complementary to the one after it and also to the fourth beatitude. I'm feeling it right now as I write these words, this verse also talks about the persecution of men against peoples and nations. In this case, it has the literal meaning of the verse, where a word can lead to painful memories for the soul, and yet, even today, it is remembered on the cross of Calvary.

How many souls are persecuted today? Well, the justice of men is very different from the loving justice of God. In spirituality, there are no harsh judgments brought about by hatred, resentment or disgust at our actions. We only have the merciful, loving and firm eyes of those who love us, but are prepared to act if our actions continue to hurt ourselves and our fellow human beings. But love always prevails in every action we take.

Those who suffer persecution because of men certainly have some light within them, and this light manifests itself in their ways and heals their fellow human beings. This word brings us this strength. For those who possess the light are indeed persecuted by those still trapped in the ignorance of love. I ask you please not to distort this wisdom, for I am not referring to the actions and consequences of our actions on the law of men. Just pray in love that those who practice iniquity will change their ways and choose love and light.

Just like those persecuted for justice, those who also suffer for love of the divine have received their reward from heaven in their death. For truly theirs is the kingdom of heaven. Light bearers will always carry their light into the world. No matter their birthplace, nationality, religion, spiritual practice, skin color, gender or anything else that might categorize a soul on this earthly plane. Their brilliance will always speak louder, their light will always shine through their actions.

That's why we see in countless religions and tales around the world avatars and examples of deities whose actions planted and harvested the sweet fruit of love. For the divine essence is always the one that stands out from the crowd, and it is the same divine essence that will always bathe in the unconditional love of the Divine Creator. Here, the light is only molded to fit into a spiritual segment, when in fact, it is always the light of the creator taking infinite forms so that no soul is left helpless, no matter where or when it was born on this Earth. Breaking the barriers of time and duality, light is in fact the most powerful and beneficial form we know.

We remember the example of Jesus, when he withdrew into the desert and was tempted by the opposite plane during his fast. At this time, Jesus had already begun his sowing on this plane, which naturally raised the attention of all the other negative souls who held dominion over peoples and nations, to pay attention to this preacher of good things and the changes that his work with spirituality would bring to this world. What they didn't expect was that even after his death, the light still shined and spread even further across this Earth.

As many pillars of light have come to this world to bring significant change through their work in union with the light. These pillars of light not only sustain this light on their journey, but their flames are spread to the people and situations around them, promoting an awakening of their consciousnesses and freeing them from aspects that no longer serve them for their highest good. In this way, the light grows, spreads and irradiates in an infinite movement. A *"butterfly"* effect where one action changes the previous and subsequent realities, which ends up bringing a lot of peace to those who receive it. When a lit candle lights an extinguished candle, that same candle can now light other candles that need its flame. Eternizing this sacred flame in this world, and becoming emissaries of the Golden Flame of Christ on this Earth.

This word teaches us that everything has a reason for happening in our lives. It shows us why we are being persecuted, and how we can get rid of this persecution and evil that is on our paths. The eighth beatitude has the power to show our good deeds, and how the paths of our existence through our good choices can change the course of our lives and bring significant changes to this world. It creates a protective shield that repels the calamities of anger, discord and injustice. It brings divine justice to its possessors, and one can call on the forces of heaven whenever celestial judgment must be present in our lives. Just as it silences in love the revolts of those who, controlled by darkness, act in profound ignorance of their actions.

The Eighth Beatitude – Seal

The Beatitudes
of Christ

שחררתם מידי החטא לכן השתעבדתם לצדקו

And having been freed from sin, you were made servants of righteousness.

Romans 6:18

שמהלהל - מיאנמה

The Ninth Beatitude

"Blessed are ye when they revile you, and persecute you, and say every evil word, being deceitful against you because of me."

Matthew 5:11

The Ninth Beatitude

"Rejoice, and be exceedingly glad, because your reward is great in the heavens, for so they persecuted the prophets before you."

Matthew 5:12

The Ninth Beatitude

Gospel of Matthew chapter 5:11-12

"Blessed are ye when they revile you, and persecute you, and say every evil word, being deceitful against you because of me."

"Rejoice, and be exceedingly glad, because your reward is great in the heavens, for so they persecuted the prophets before you."

Sacred Mantra: *OM – Ah – Heh – Vah – Heh – Kah – Lah – Mah – Hah – Yeh – Shuh – Ah. OM – Yeh – Mah – Lah – Hah – Yeh – Mah – Tah – Mah – Yeh – Shuh – Ah.*

Sacred Mantra: *OM – Ah – Kah – Yeh – Vah – Ah – Vah – Ah – Vah -Kah – Rah – Vah – Yeh – Shuh – Ah. OM – Mah – Yeh – Vah – Vah – Mah – Uh – Mah – Rah – Lah – Ah – Yah – Yeh – Shuh – Ah.*

Candle color: *White, yellow or gold.*

Crystal: *Citrine.*

In the Old Testament, we can see various trials that the prophets who preceded Jesus went through. Trials that are still remembered today, such as Daniel in the lions' den, a true test of faith and perseverance. He was not helpless even in the fiery furnace. The book of Daniel seems to have a magical force so great, so strong, that you feel it when you open the chapter.

When we touch Daniel's energy, we feel such a solar wave, and at the same time, a serenity from heaven. There are many mysteries hidden in this book, mysteries that long to be revealed to humanity. Daniel, in his many visions, was a prophet, king and servant of the Lord. Graced by his incomparable devotion, he had the presence of the Holy Angels and Archangels in his life. I see the strength of the Archangel Michael with him, as well as Gabriel, Raphael and Uriel. Daniel, a kindred soul, an example to be given and followed, of whom his faith and devotion are still manifest in our midst, who in eternal grace, still remains.

How many times have you experienced any kind of persecution, attack or insult because of the good you do for this world? Your work, your existence, the good you do, every light you share, whichever path you choose, has certainly planted wonderful seeds that germinate into true love.

In particular, I don't like or approve of the idea that, in order to be emissaries of the light, we have to suffer for it. However, it is a reality that still persists in many good people in this world. The lack of knowledge and appropriate tools can be a key factor between a peaceful life and a life of hardship in the face of the actions of men and darkness.

I myself have been between the two paths, and today I realize that a lot could have been avoided if only I had the light of knowledge and discernment to know what comes from the light and what comes from the darkness. If we apply the tools that spirituality gives us in the right way and walk on the right paths, we will certainly be able to live a more harmonious and peaceful life, without the great persecutions of this Earth, and in fact alleviate any conflicts that may occur. However, we need to stay on the paths of evolution, understanding, wisdom and a greater comprehension of our earthly existence, so that we can always evolve and constantly improve ourselves, and never go backwards on our journey. In this way, everything we plan to do in this world will come to fruition.

Looking back, I see that spirituality has always given me the tools to make my dreams and goals come true, and at the end of the day, it's up to me to know how to use correctly all the infinite intuitions and messages that have been provided by heaven's love.

Many places where love is truly preached, welcoming truth and sincere devotion, they teach us to be better every day. These places carry out tremendous spiritual work and, with every soul that passes through them, love, light and charity are spread through the lives that have been supported by the spirituality of that place. Good mediums and their psychic tools, if used wisely, are instruments of the divine light, which manifests on this Earth to show a path that people trapped in their afflictions cannot see. Just as Christ said:

"Come to me, all you who labor and are heavy laden, and I will give you rest." Matthew 11:28

Christ, supported by mentors, doctors and healers, worked together to heal those souls. Christ, aware of how much spirituality was active in his life, was an instrument of healing, devotion and the spread of light on this Earth. That's why he was able to perform his miracles, cures and support all those souls who came to him, seeking an end to their earthly pain. Christ's spirituality was what we might call an infinite legion of light. I close my eyes and see spirits covered in luminosity, radiant like the sun, in an incomparable colored white light. This same light was present in his preaching, in his beatitudes, in his words, in his healings and in his actions during his so tenuous time on this earth.

From light to light, Christ lit up many unlit souls, who in turn were able to light up other souls when they were healed. And in this process of endless healing, he was able to ascend to heaven and rule on his rightful divine throne, due to his countless actions for the good of humanity and many planetary spheres that we still don't know about. You only ascend by merit; lineage, blood and recommendations are nothing more than sand in the wind. As fleeting as a breath of life, they have no value in the eyes of the Creator.

Going back a little to the words of the beatitude, when Christ said that we are blessed because of the persecution in his name, he reveals to us that we are persecuted precisely because of the light and love we carry. We know that whoever follows the light becomes more light. Christ, being a bearer of the light, and this light being propagated in our bodies out of love and respect for his path, we will then be targets of that which is contrary to the light. Being contrary to it, opposition is formed against the divine plans. From this opposition, many souls suffer because of their missions. I know this may resonate a little with you, or perhaps it describes your current situation.

Understanding this, I want everyone to know that yes, it is possible to live a full, peaceful and abundant life. To do this, we must work on our inner selves and correctly apply the tools given to us to raise our vibration and, consequently, raise our standard of living to a more fulfilling and happier reality. The famous *"Shifting"*, much talked about abroad, which consists of changing our reality, is nothing more than changing our vibratory pattern. This book, these rituals and these beatitudes come from heaven to do just that. It comes to help us change our frequency in order to achieve more beautiful realities and the fullness of unconditional Christic love in our lives.

This beatitude brings us profound revelations of our good in this world. It is similar to its predecessor in that its energy is interconnected with the last one, starting from the same principle, the same mouth and the same light that was uttered. It reveals to us the knowledge of all that we are in this world. It reveals to us what changes we have come to make on this Earth and teaches us how to exercise this divine office that was given to us and requested by ourselves before incarnation, in order to fulfill this sacred and heavenly mission. It opens up ways for us to be better and makes us understand the reasons for persecution against us. It also shows us how to get rid of them. You can meditate and ask for deliverance from them, as well as pray for protection so that no harm comes to your life.

The Ninth Beatitude - Seal

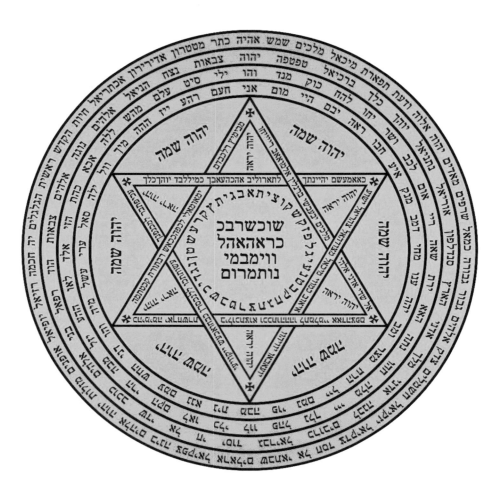

Yeshua Hamashiach - Seal

The Seal of All the Beatitudes

This is the seal of all the beatitudes, it has all the verses in Hebrew of the words of the beloved Lord Jesus. This seal can be used to conquer all the qualities of the beatitudes, just as it is used to connect with Christ and his divine radiance in the Sermon on the Mount.

Use the Golden Star, the activation of the beatitudes or whatever practices you wish to connect with the beloved Lord Yeshua Hamashiach.

Walking in the Holy Light

Walking in the light is an eternal process. Just as the path of this book is also a journey worthy of many stories and tales to be passed on to all the hearts that have come this far. Your path in this book will always be watered by love and you will always have the support of spirituality on your paths. We know that it is difficult, at certain times, to remain uplifted, vibrating in love and attuned to something greater in your lives. But don't give up, I know that the angels will always be with you.

This book is the work of a journey, and should be taken with you on your own journey. Here, you can find insights into solving your daily problems or those that have been lingering for a long time in your life. As it is a journey, I encourage you, the reader, to dedicate yourself to manifesting Christ's beatitudes in your life. One meditation a day, one contact a day can make great transformations in your existence in this world. A gradual, deep and lasting healing process.

As I said earlier, the light comes to those who come to it. Therefore, there is nothing to fear, because in the light we always find security, peace, victory, healing, love, mercy, prosperity, protection, elevation and the ascension of our souls to new paths of existence and goodness.

The Beatitudes should be shared with everyone around you. That's why I also encourage you to share your experiences and, above all, the words of Christ with your fellow human beings. We know that Christ is always present on our paths, and he is always present when we talk about him. Jesus, in his most perfect love, is always present at all times. And I know that a sweet smile is present at this very moment, as you read these words, and feel this faint and pure love enveloping you.

Writing this book has been a long process, between stops, comings and goings, and finally it has come to an end. It's been a warm journey, but at the same time it's been full of challenges and tests that I've had to go through with a lot of wisdom and intelligence. Among the balance of temperance in my life, I could see when I channeled these words from a kind, pure and loving spirit of light. That these words could bring light into the lives of those who need it.

I know that Christ's beatitudes can bring about profound inner and planetary changes with their deep healing techniques. We know that nothing exists but light. And by expanding that light into this world, we are being Christic pillars of strength, will, wisdom, love, ascension, healing, truth, devotion, transmutation and mercy in this world.

When the light of Christ spreads more and more over this earth, we will be able to see this world become more subtle. Wars will come to an end, hunger will cease to exist, and control will lose its strength, just blowing away like dust in the wind. The light takes hold of every heart and soul in this world. We acquire a cosmic and planetary consciousness and we know our place, our mission and our role as human beings and as spirits residing in this planetary sphere.

In this incarnation, we can be better, we can do better, we can be who we are, free of all illusions, regrets, guilt, fears and karmas. We can only be light. And in this kind and sweet light, we are complete in truth, complete in unconditional love, complete with the Creator, complete in everything, simply complete in our existence. The touch of the stars is at our fingertips, contact with other civilizations is made instantaneously, and intergalactic travel is as common and pleasurable in our world as the sweet singing of birds at our window. The love of the greater spirits is felt in every breath taken into our lungs.

Although it is a true utopia, it is projected and is already being realized here in this world. A dream not so far away, true, not false, real and tangible. Strong and not weak, courageous and not fearful. Subtle and not rough, peaceful and harmonious. I know that this world to come is already present on our paths, I know that it's already here right now, I know that it's just an inch away from our hands. You just have to feel it, just tune in, and it will magically become present. Regeneration is often seen as painful, but pain need never be obligatory, it is simply a choice, a path to be traveled by souls who lack the knowledge of love. Be it guilt, remorse or fear, things so temporal that they cease to exist on a new Earth. A new dawn, a new day, a new sunrise with all its completeness in perfect, heavenly love.

When the sun shines and we feel its warmth on our skin, when the winds bring peace and tranquility, when the earth rests and begins to bear fruit, when silence is present in the big cities, when we can hear the songs of the birds around our house, when the water flows pure into the oceans, and it moves so calmly in harmony with the dance of the winds, when the trees bear their succulent fruit in full abundance, when drought ceases to exist, and the sands give way to vegetation and the life that will sprout there, when the animals no longer die to humans and live in peace on their lands, when the skies open up and the clouds reflect the sun's rays over the hills, and a sweet heavenly blue covers this world, we will know that this long-awaited day has arrived. And from that moment on, we will know that we live in a new world. A new day is knocking at our door, may we be prepared to welcome it with open arms. Blessed be God, who brings his love, and who brings his blessed son for a new dawn here on this earth.

May Christ's beatitudes illuminate your paths, heal your pain, shine his mercies in your hearts, and open a new life to all who come here. Fraternal peace and light. - Rodrigo Bispo Carvalho.

Additional Information

       In this chapter I've provided a QR Code for downloading all the seals of the beatitudes that have been passed on here in high resolution. All you have to do is click on the link, download it and use it as you see fit in your daily practices. If you point your cell phone camera at the image below, a link will appear that will take you to the download of the blessed seals. Use a QR Code reader if you need to. You can also ask me for the access link via the email address provided on the next page.

*Qr Code to download the
Beatitudes*

Final notes

Thank you for buying an official copy of this book, it motivates me to bring you more content and enables me to launch new books on this subject. I hope you get great results and change your life for the better. If you would like to send me any feedback, opinions or have found any errors in the book, please send me an e-mail to: **arsauroradawn@gmail.com**

Remember to rate the book on amazon or whatever official platform you bought it on. Your stars and comments are extremely important to me.

If you want to join the chain of good dharma, post about the book on your social networks, you'll be helping many people get to know this work, and possibly helping all of them on their earthly journeys.

Many blessings upon you, Ars Aurora.

Follow me on the social medias:

Amazon Author Page

Instagram

Facebook Profile

Facebook Page

Facebook Group

Patreon

Printed in France by Amazon
Brétigny-sur-Orge, FR